THE ETERNAL DARK

B

Andrew Brenza

Unsolicited Press
Portland, Oregon
www.unsolicitedpress.com
info@unsolicitedpress.com
619–354–8005

Distributed by Asterism Books
https://asterismbooks.com/

For wholesale orders:
Asterism Books
568 1st Avenue South, Ste 120
Seattle, WA 98104
(206) 485-4829
info@asterismbooks.com

Cover Design: Kathryn Gerhardt
Editor: Summer Stewart

et al.

a poem etched from *the eternal dark*

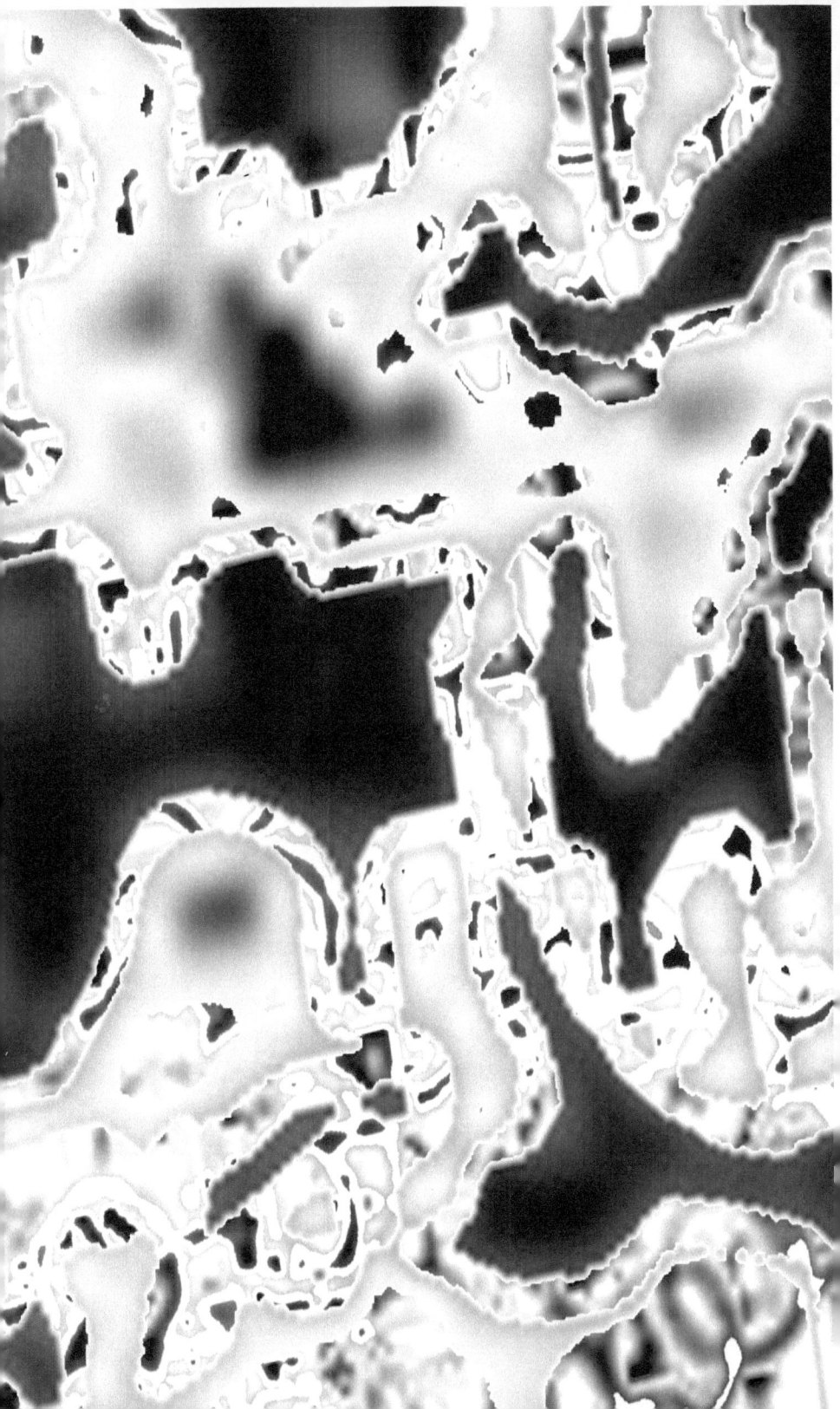

web. That is what it was trying to show you yester-
day."

Moor, still sitting at the base of the tree,
leaned back and took a deep breath, the memory fad-
ing. Then, glancing down at her hand, she pressed her
fingers into the soil of the forest floor. Digging
gently, she closed her eyes, and tried to sing. But,
the Song of Power would not come. The melody had van-
ished from her mind, though she could still feel it
there, just below her awareness, like a boulder bo-
ried by stone. Moor had shattered, broken. Frantic-
ally she grasped at it, trying to wrest it from the
tip of her tongue. But the song refused to budge,
though it wouldn't disappear. Rather it hung like a
hole in space, the vague memory of its existence
serving as reminder of what was lost. Moor's spirit
collapsed. Her eyes glazed over, and her gaze fixed
emptily on the distance. Her thoughts grew thin and
ghostly, devoid of purpose. But she did not weep. The
devastation of this last loss had pushed her beyond
sorrow into a ... oblivion. Now, she sat numbly on the
forest floor, staring into the distance as the light
ca...ed and night began to fall. Her breath grew slow
and deep, her mind grew dark and unresponsive.

And she waited. She waited despite the uncom-
fortable stillness that filled her body as the dark
woods grew loud with the strange and frightening
sounds of night. Hour after hour, she waited for
herself, she waited for anything. Moor knew not, un-
til, at some point, she slowly rose like a creeping
vine to her feet. Then, there she stood, unperturbed,

...ability her mother might ... her ... out, to tell her it was in her head. The conflict between ... board of doubt left Noor feeling, on the one hand, defensive and ... about her **impressions and** ... about her mother's **motivations** on the other. So, day by day Noor's fears and anxiety increased. ... ahead of the Archetype, she was now likely ... hard to ... her mother at once and to ... herself. She was even becoming resentful of her mother's lack of improvement. Likely, Noor reasoned, the Archetype had permanently damaged her mother, ... her ... **insurmountably,** and had thus trapped her in the cottage. It was **obvious** to Noor that her mother ... did not have **the strength to flee.** Instead, the day was now **stuck in** the cottage waiting for the Archetype to finish them off. She wondered how it her mother was, in fact, working toward this end. Not ... or ... be aware of the Archetype's manipulations. Had it ... that her mother was still so weak, even after a month and a half of rest. Noor found it hard to accept, ... see ... the lingering effects of the encounter, herself.

Noor knew these thoughts were **conjectures that** could even be the result of her own ... Nevertheless, the **ambiguity made** it impossible to act, to make a decision. As each day passed, she felt that her and her mother's safety depended on their ability to flee the cottage, to get out before the Archetype returned. Yet she could not see how that would be **possible** with her mother in such a weak state. She doubted her ability to take care of her ...

dead. I could see large gashes across each of their
bodies, terror opened along the rib cage. What skin
they had was blackened, as though burned, or not
washed. Their eyes were hollowed out, and their
flesh drawn taut, desiccated, and without sheen. Yet,
despite the disfigurement, there was something familiar
about the man's sunken and mutilated visage. I
felt, with a sense of panic, that I had seen it be-
fore, a long time ago. It seemed to dredge up like a
ghost from the dark recesses of my tortured imagina-
tion, but I couldn't pin it down. Besides, more than
anything, I was overcome with horror and sadness for
the family.

          Placing a hand on the man's chest, I lowered my
head and prayed. But the moment I touched him, some-
thing happened. In an instant, everything went dark
and then, as though I were looking through a tunnel,
I was cast the door of the bedroom and pulled out.
I felt the thinness and weakness of mortal flesh and
the pall of grief. I saw a darkened hall lined with
flashing into the long dark room, and there, the sil-
houette of someone I knew, my brother, maybe, emerging
from the shadow and walking towards my side. I
watched as the door unfolded, and as, before
ones, my little boy carved before me. I watched as the
darkness fed the thirst of some evil and bottomless
entity in this world. And then, the dark room me, and
fell into darkness into darkness, torn out of their
bodies, strangled on the shadow, and sucked. The
drowning dead and dead to the edge of oblivion,
death, where I could flee and eat the time.

...of death. Noor had no knowledge of anyone of
... Then the meaning of the vision dawned on her.
... that she had witnessed was the Archetype taking the
life of this woman's child. She and the woman had
been forced to watch. Yet, it happened in such a way
that it seemed to be Noor's doing. A terrible fear
consumed her. And pain... her body felt as though it
were on fire. Looking down, she saw the markings left
of the Archetype glowing softly but horridly. It was
a sickening sight, but Noor tried to get control of
herself, of the situation.

"It wasn't...," began Noor. But the woman inter-
rupted. The suddenness and depth of her horror and
of ... had sent her into a frenzy.

"I had no choice. I had to come here. He was
going to die, but then you wouldn't let go," she
cried. "I tried to pull away, but you wouldn't ...
no." She was standing now, ... to ..., ...
... Noor, ... eyed with horror and disbelief.

"I didn't do it," Noor blurted in panic. "It
was...the Archetype!" Yet, as Noor ... the
fate of the creature, she then now hoped that all
... She knew the woman, even if she were able to
..., would not believe her, would not know ... that
she was a ... perceiving, how that she was ... in
... , there was nothing Noor could do. The people of
the village had never encountered anything like the
Archetype, and, even if they could be convinced of
its existence, they would likely blame the ... her
for summoning it.

..., I understood what ...

... feeding ...

... wrought ...

... I also knew ... the ...

... physical presence would ...

... set itself up as a healer ...

... fallen into communal despair ...

Archetype remained in the village. ███████████ net-
work showed no change in its whereabouts, while the
earth beneath the town ████████████ with ████████
████████ this was discouraging. Likely this meant
that any alteration in the villagers' attitude **toward**
me was simply **incidental** to whatever changes the Ar-
chetype had wrought for i**tself.** ████████ a great calm
had fallen over the settlement. Although the late
summer days were mild, **the sun low** and dim, and the
fields **heavy with grain,** the farmers had forsaken
their work. No longer had they reason to the
roof, and they do not seem to be preparing for the
harvest. It was then, though, that I could have sur-
mised that the farmers had gone about even the most
basic matter of survival.

        I began to worry. Foremost in my mind was the
possibility the Archetype ███████████████████████. In-
stead of attacking me directly, an approach that had
up until that point always failed, perhaps it had
thought of something else. Perhaps it knew of or
guessed at my concern for the townsfolk and was hop-
ing to exploit it. Perhaps it deemed the best way to
get to me was not **by hunting** and traed me out by
turning me onto the open against my will, where I
would then be exposed and vulnerable to all manner of
attack. And, perhaps, it knew the best way to out
me into the open was to attack the townsfolk and to
harm **the unsuspecting,** capitalizing my sense of
justice and my duty then to protecting those in
need.

        Perhaps, though, I ███ • • ● ███ the Archetype

At least, now, the pain had re-eased, and along with it, the deadair. Somehow, she was herself again. Somehow, despite her despair and now the numbing dreadfulness, she had come through it. Noor decided to let the woman in.

Opening the door, she saw a short but solid creature wrapped in layers of dark cloth, her face obscured by a long, handwoven shawl, one hand clutching it to her throat, **holding it tight**. On seeing Noor, the woman startled, and jumped back from the door. She **seemed about to run**, and when Noor looked into her eyes, she saw a wild fear there, fear bordering on disbelief. But she also saw the woman's desperate determination. Thus, the pair, facing each other in the **light cast through the doorway**, regarded one another for a long silent moment. Then, the woman spoke.

"A-a-are you the Witch of the Wood," she stammered timidly. Then, seemingly afraid and ashamed of her presumption, the woman lowered her eyes and bowed her head. Noor felt sorry for her. **The totality of her was pathetic**. Yet, the question also held a certain danger that stirred Noor's suspicions. In truth, Noor was not, in fact, the Witch of the Wood. Her **mother** was. Noor couldn't help wondering if the woman were **fishing for** information, assessing the strength of the witches' positions.

But Noor wanted to avoid **any appearance of weakness**, especially regarding her mother's slow recovery. Perhaps it had been many years since she had allowed herself to be seen by the villagers —

felt happy in the gentle waves of its passage, and she surrendered it willingly, her spirit in a state of relaxed attention. Then, a voice emerged.

"Thank you," it said thinly, without being loud. It seemed to come from nowhere and everywhere at once, emerging like a thought in Koo's mind, and sounding like an echo in Koo's ears.

"Who's there?" Koo replied, looking frantically for the voice's owner. But in the rush of varicolored light Koo saw no one. Instead, she began to see shapes form in the dancing light. A little by little, as though wind were blowing too off a distant shore, Koo saw petals drifting on the dark, tending to the soil. There was the stream purling peacefully, and she heard herself singing the song of power, harmonizing now with the song of the trees. Amazed by the song's beauty, or the beauty of her own voice, heard now for the first time as though it were someone else's, Koo's heart was bad. She felt a longing to hold that beauty, a stilling of the dark, to comfort her, to protect her.

"I am here," came the answer. "I have always been here, and will always be." Again, there was no one. But Koo remained calm. Although reluctantly, somehow she accepted the situation of her predicament. Rather, Koo felt a deep peace as she watched the dancing of the light, and more through the working. Soon, and Koo began to, she could see the warmth of the air. She'd been told to keep waiting, the arriving of this glow of her own side, and her spirit reopened. Then, to her astonishment, she watched and she dance on the world's

..., a ...ed ... the ... ...ld ... ...s.
B... ...a... ...differe..., ...ld a.. ... ...ea
... ...e ..., a... ...ad ... ...ad ... ...o... ...
... ...ad ...e... ... ...co... ... ...ood... ...
...al...e..., ...t ....d ... ...ee ... ...ea..., ...e
...ld a... ...ee ....o...... ... ...ea..., ...ld
...ee ... ..., pensive a... a ..., ...a... ... ...
... ...oo... ..., as ...e strangeness ...e... ...e ...d, ...e
... ...ed ... ...e...ed ... ...e ... ...e
a... ...e... ...a...e ....ee... ...e ...a...ad... ...o... ...a... ...a...
...oo...... ... ..., ...e...e ... ...e ...o... ...ld,
...a...d ... ...e...o...e ...e... ...a... ...e ...o..., ...e ... a... ...
...e ...a... ....e, ... a...o...... ...a...
...o... a ...o... ...o...e..., ...o ... a...d ... ...e...a...ed ...a... o...
..., ...oo... ... ...ea... o... ...e... ... ...e, ...a... ... ...
...... a... o... ...a... ...oo... a... o...e...... ... a ....
...e ... ...e. " ... ...o...," ...oo ...a...d, ...ee... ... ...e
...oo... a... ... . " ... a... ...a...a..," ...e ... ...e ...o...... ...ed.
...e..., o... ... ..., a... ...o... a... ... .o... ...ed ... ...
a... ...ed... ... ...e ...a... ...o...e..., ...e... movements coor-
dinated by a single will, ...oo... ...e...a...ed, a ....e
...o... ....e... ...o..., " ... a... ...a...a..," a...d ...e ...a... ...o...
a...e...ed a... ... ...e ...a...o... ...o... ...e ...o...e... . " ... a...
...o...... ."

. . . . .

I left the shadows o... ...e ...e... ... ... o...e ...a...
a... a ...e, ...a... ...o... ...ed ... .e...ed ...o ...ee ...a...
...a...e. ... ...e...ed ...o ...ee the wound that haunted ....
...a... o... the woods. ...... o...a... ... ...o...e... ... ...o...e ..., ...
...ad ...o ...o...ed the remnants of a scream ...o ....e...
...oo... ...o..., ...a... ...a a... ...ed, ...o... ...ee ...e ...e...a...e

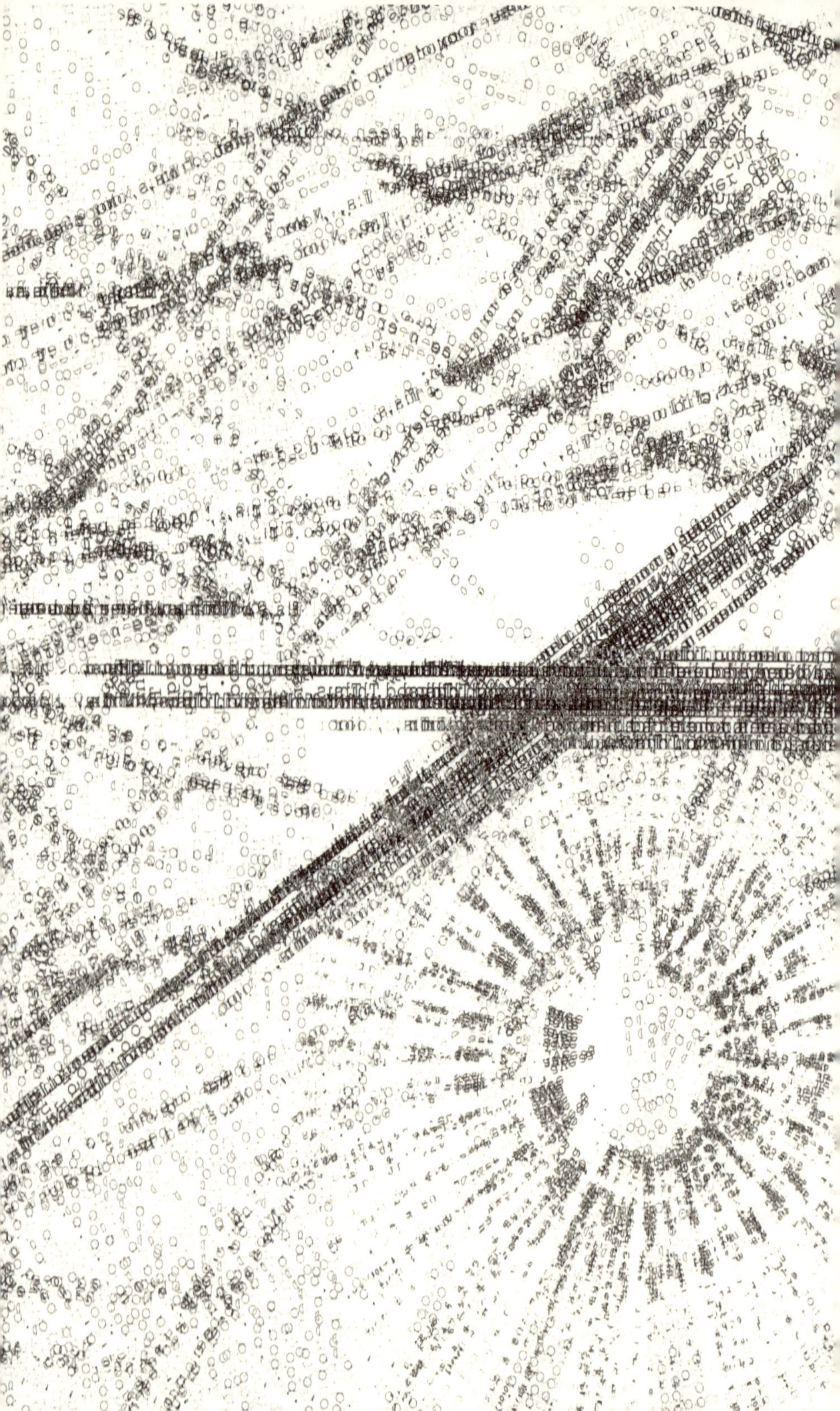

The song had ceased by strange and unwelcome noises blinking through the trees thinking, *I will fight it.* B

I slithered I approached.

window of a

"I can feel it," said the woman, closing her eyes. "I know it in my heart. He will not get better without help."

"Good. Now, give me your hands and show me," answered Noor, extending her palms, face up, towards the woman. The woman looked at them cautiously. But after a short hesitation, she reciprocated, laying both hands in Noor's. Noor felt the woman's cold skin against her own and shuddered. There was something horrible about the sensation, something death-like. But Noor allowed the sensation to pass through her without resistance and soon it was gone. She was then able to gauge her reactions to accept the woman as she was, without judgement. She knew this was the only way to understand the woman's predicament, to understand what was happening to her son. Noor's mother had taught her the technique, and Noor had practiced it many times...on animals, on plants, but never on a human. With her mother to aid her, Noor had learned to place her hands in the earth and to open herself to the movement and condition of the mycelial network. In this way she had learned to hear the voice of the forest, to see out of the forest's eyes, sometimes witnessing events in other worlds away. Her, being a totally, she had never heard a human thirst, not until lately, at least. The prospect was intoxicating. She did not know what to expect.

And Noor closed her eyes and waited. But, instead of the woman's thoughts, her sensations of something shot up her arms. Noor winced, wanting to pull away. But she didn't dare do. She couldn't. Something

the distance between us. This also meant I had to be more cautious. I felt certain that the Archetype had about kind of me and knew I was in pursuit of it, or aware of the threat, the Archetype's blood and seemed to thicken and slowed. Hard to deal with, the tracks were now partially obscured, and I wondered if this was intentional. I wondered if the Archetype were trying to lead me into an ambush. Fearful of this, I had to slow my pace as well, stopping often to assess all, or to send myself ahead before the rest of me would follow.

However, my concerns about ambush quickly abated. Two kilometers from the site of the second habitation, I came upon the body of the bear. There on the ground, in a horrible heap of singed fur and bloody flesh, lay the remains of the bear, battered to nothing. I could tell the Archetype had used just enough power, exerted just enough time, to kill it, but nothing more. It had not fed on the bear as the burns were far from complete. This was simply an act of murder. Because of the cruel senselessness after so much abuse, this scene was the most upsetting I had come across. It seemed plain to me that, if the Archetype was indeed done with the bear, it could have released the bear back into the forest. Based on everything it had been through, the bear would likely have died anyway, but, at least, it would not have been pointlessly murdered.

Rage welled in me. More than anything, I wanted to make the Archetype as much as it had harmed this animal. I wanted to make it suffer and suffer and

their spells but open to the traditional purpose, the visitors sat rapt in the audience beyond their... afford no eye contact, pretend to be somewhere else, or something weeping solibly.

Sometimes, however, especially while mother and daughter sang, Noor wanted something more than fear and ● ● ●● ... ●● ...ess, something far later. Sitting on her bed in the dark, waiting for their latest visitor to arrive, Noor remembered the expression of some, those departing that had glanced obliquely in the thin pool that somehow came free, suddenly touching with **livid** face and fearful eyes, sudden-strong anger. Noor remembered while standing near, all seemed of **beseeching**, aloud no request. It, bitterly, under their **breath**, loathing yet something for her mother's fate. She recalled with pearls on the **ill-hidden waves of** almost that lapsed a long sore near tony' face, as the froth soon opened and that were hunted inside. She pledged to remember the encountered roaming or some who revealed the **need** to hear her mother's vocal of the recool, of her **moth**er's **song**.

Her her mother always ●● ●● ... opened about this from time to time, but she never openly questioned the practice. Inherently, she seemed **to understand the obligation.** It was woven, **in the fabric of things,** and so Noor would do that had required of her. Besides, no matter how it came, no matter seeing to see, Noor ultimately believed that the power of her mother's magic would protect her. Now that she had been brought still so to her own.

... attention, ...

... self, ...

... the back of her head ...

... a great snake ... squeezing ...

... a shadowy appendage ...

...again, pulling myself close. There I lay for a long time, partly too sore to move, partly too weak to get up, but also ...ored in the multilayered warmth ...... of my manifold body. There, on the ground .... of the hollow of the dead maple tree, I lay, aching, too damaged to worry about danger, and dreamed.

I dreamed of running and running and running, of soaring over rock and bole, brook and stream, joy in my heart. I dreamed of the ...... of my paths, ... forest and ..... of .... valley, all at once. ...... of the thrill of smelling kilometers into the land with a single breath of ...... in all directions with a single glance. I dreamed of trapping a roebuck at a river's edge, lithe as anything, ... in the power of my mind and body, the reach of my perceptions, and the strength of .....

.... at the same time, I also dreamed of my ...... I saw her .... glowing in the after ...... of ......, and ...... a kind hand on my cheek as I lay in a warm bed by a warm fire. I dreamed of her ...... gently washing over me as we sat .... into enchanted .... And I saw the ...... in her eyes.

It was ■ lovely ......, complete in its .... But soon enough, I woke with a start, ... to be fearful of the possibility of danger around me. .... the pain in my body, my limbs throbbing with soreness, I forced my attention

... incandescent worms throughout ...

... a wild stream of recollections ...

... an approaching visitor ... the hopeless desire, ... a ghost in her mind. ...

"Please," _____ _____, "_____ _____. There
_____ _____ _____. B_____ was too
_____. A _____ _____, _____, _____
_____, _____ _____ _____
_____ _____, _____ _____. _____
_____ _____, _____ decline, _____
_____ _____ _____ _____
_____, _____ _____ A _____
_____ attack.

_____ silence _____, _____ _____
_____ fatigue. _____ _____
_____ A _____ _____
_____, _____ _____. _____
_____, _____ _____ _____
_____ _____, _____ _____.
_____ _____ _____ _____
_____. _____ _____ _____

and intimately, _____ _____ _____
_____. _____ _____ _____,
_____ _____ _____, _____, _____
_____. _____ _____ A _____?
_____ _____, _____, _____
_____ _____, _____ _____ _____
_____ _____ _____ _____?

_____ _____ _____ _____
_____, _____ _____, _____.
_____ _____ _____ _____.
_____? _____ _____ A _____
_____ _____, _____ _____.
_____ _____ A _____ _____.

mind, Loor's mind snapped shut and she was gone.

Blackness. Stillness. Without evil. But then—
pain, like the redoubt between free roots. And the
feeling of something hard against her face. Pain...
In the distance, a gurgle of noises, growing closer.
Loor tried to move. Pain coursing through her body.
Weakness in her legs and ▮▮▮▮▮. An increasing isolat-
ion. ▮▮▮▮▮▮ Loosening. Tears. But the noises
growing louder still. Nearer now. Her skin burning
with a wild pain. But the noises. They were now her
mother's voice. Shouting. Blasting. Nearer. She too
in pain. The feeling of the floor against Loor's
face. The odd texture. Revealing. Outline of bed and
chair. Outline of wall and door. Light coming near-
er. Shadow moving in the next room. Loud voices.
Nearer now. The shouting of her mother and the Ar-
chetype. The walls shaking. The floor trembling. Loor
rising to her feet, pain surging in her muscles.
Her voice screaming, feeling the weight of her body,
feeling the pain of the injured and the fear of
death. Rising to help her mother. Standing now.
Panting. Strength returning. A red rage swelling in
her heart. A red rage directed at the Archetype. Rage
and now. Rising to the bedroom door. Running to
door...

In the middle of the living room, Loor's mother
fought the Archetype, who had, in the guise of the
alter ego, been damaged and altered in form. Loor
pushed at the bedroom door. The creature's head had been
bent inward so that its skull had snapped. The
head was now flush with its shoulder, forming a sharp

...to manipulate...

...a matter of degree...

...holes...

...in the dark... profoundly vulnerable...

...the violence... of the darkness around... her thoughts...

was worn out from the journey and experiences of the previous day. **I just didn't have it in me** to look for a more suitable spot. In any case, **when I heard the** door barking and **yapping**, they weren't close. But they were approaching, so I knew they were following my scent. Irritated, I **rose and shook the sleep from** my fur and limbs. I then reached into the dark, a facet stretched long, to watch them. I saw they had formed a long line of tougher and door, headed in my direction, presumably after a man I might also catch and get behind them. Even still, I was surprised. There were **more men** and more door **than I had ex**pected. It seemed the Architype's poison had worked quickly; the group was large, organized and clear in its purpose.

But staying ahead of them was easy. Men are slow and clumsy in the **woods,** and their door, those fat and silly things, are too. So, despite their numbers, I wasn't worried. I knew I could outpace them, which I easily did, always staying a few hundred meters ahead of the door's incessant yapping. My plan was simply to outrun them, **to keep a safe distance** until they grew bored and tired of the hunt and went home. I even altered my shape at times, **to frustrate the ease of their** tracking. On one occasion I separated myself into two bodies, one of which **stuck** to the current **trajectory** while the other went wildly off to the side, circling here and there and then continuing further before returning. It almost made me laugh to hear the door running off in so many odd directions.

"They do not understand _____ .."

"Do_' they know I want to ___ ___ ___ ."

"___ ___ , ___ , _ think they do. But they are afraid o_ o__ oo__ , _o__ oo__ , __ __ __ ___ ___ ___o_ __o__ . __e ___a__ a_e a__a__ __e__ _o__ a__a_o."

"_ _e_ a__ _ _o, _oo, _o__ ___ . _ _e _e_ they throw _o ___ ."

"B__ , ___ love, _o__ a_e _o_ ___a__ . _o_e , a__ _e ___o__ _o__ ___a_ _o__ a_e ." _o__o _oo_ _e__ _o _e_ _o__e_ a__ __e _a___ __a_ o_ __e _o_e__ __oo_ . "___e __e _o__ _a__, " _a__ _oo_'_ _o__e_ . ___ , _oo_'_ _o__e_ __a__e_ _oo_'_ e___e__e_ _a__ a__ __o____ __ __ __e __ea___ . _a____o _oo_'_ _a__ _o___ on the ground, _oo_'_ _o__e_ __o_e_ _e_ ___e___ _e__ee_ _e_ _a__o__ _a___ , a__ _o_e__e_ they dug into the damp dirt of __e _o_e__ __oo_ . ___ _o__e_ __ea__ _o __o_ a _a__ o_ __e _o__ __a_ _oo_ _a__ _e__e_ _ea_o.

"___o_e _o__ e_e_ , my love, " ___ __e__e_ _oo_'_ _o__e_ , a__ _oo_ _o_e_e_ , rapt by _e_ _o__e_'_ _o__e . __e_ ___e __e_ __e structure o_ __e_ _a__ __ea__ __o __a__e_ . __ _e_ ___o'_ e_e , __e _a_ __e_ ___ _e__ _a__e_ _a_e and __e_ __e_ . ___e _a__ _ea _e_ a__e__ __o __e _a____ a_ , ___ _a__o____ , __e_ twisted around the growing and spreading _o___ o_ _e_ _o__e_'_ _a__ . ___ _ , _o_e__e_ , _o__e_ a__ _a__o__e_ _ea___ _e__e_ _ee_e_ __o __e __o___ , __e__ _a__o _o___ o__ o_ a ___e __ __e __ o__a__ _o soil. B__ __e_ , __e_ ___o__e_ , a_e__ _o__e_ , a__ __a__e_ . A _o__ ___ __e__e _o _o__e_ .

__o____ , as though _a__ a_a__ , _oo_ __ea__ _o _ee_ _o__e____o . A_ ___ __ , _ tickled _e_ __a__ , a__ __e__

There, like a cloud in a windless sky, she lingered,
one gust away from total dispersal, one strong breeze
from personal annihilation.

Yet, just before she could return to the anonymous All, Noor would suddenly decide to walk again as inexplicably as she had stopped. Balanced on the knife edge of the abyss, Noor lifted her feet, one by one, cracking the joints at her toes and heels, and moved forward. The numbness at her fingertips stopped, and the pall that had settled over her joints dwindled away. Awkwardly, yet purposefully, the ancient and grinding journey now resumed, Noor curled somewhere within herself, unaware of danger, unafraid of death, and oblivious to pain, grief and fear. On and on, she wandered, day after day, week after week. It was a trek without direction, without purpose, but relentless, the skin on the soles of Noor's shoes and feet growing harder and darker from wear.

But she wasn't always unconscious. From time to time, just as abruptly as the stopping and starting, Noor became self-aware. Like waking up in a strange room after a too-long sleep, she looked at her surroundings in confusion and terror. The forest appeared unfamiliar and unrecognizable as she realized she had no memory of how or why she had come to the place she now found herself. Even stranger, while coming to, she sometimes found herself and rose as if only she had no recollection of beginning. At those moments of coming to, she would find herself lying on the bank of a forest stream, or walking waist-deep and drifting deeply. Other times she found

..........ed, ... ly in the heavy ....
of the .... moon, and the air was ...... But most
importantly, ... the ...... were at their ......,
I would have ...... as I made my way to the edge of
town. This pleased me. ..., before ....
entirely to the approach, I .... a ...... into ..
the ..... of barley that lay .... ahead. ......
...., I .... into it, smelling as I went, ...
... nothing until the field abruptly ..... well be-
fore .... it should.

There, before me, I saw a large portion of the
field had been cleared of ...... In its place were a
...... of low mounds with .... I recognized ....
as ...... like the one I dug for Dial. Suddenly, I
was aware of the odor of fresh death. I ...., re-
turning to the cover of the high grass, ... and
whimpering. I wanted to run from this place. I wanted
to ..... the clear evil that ...... there. But I
forced myself to stay. I forced myself to ......,
hidden in the grass, and to observe. But nothing
moved and nothing stirred, and no ....
.... my nose.

.... the area was safe for the moment,
so I advanced entirely into it. What I found sickened
and .... There were between 10 to 20 graves in
the area, and of them ....., the earth still dark and
damp over them, visibly so, even in the dim
moonlight. By their ....., it appeared that most of
the graves were for children: babies and toddlers,
through young adolescents. However, a few of the smaller
graves were also ones nearly the size of adult

angle with the creature's shoulders, looking straight up, mouth gaping open, while its body stood upright. However, out of the mouth, a shadow head had emerged. Covered in yellow eyes, its **mouth** was full of screaming blood and flame within, opened at Noor's mother. Shadowy tentacles extended from the body of the old ... and were now **pinning** Noor's mother to the wall of the front door. **In terror,** she saw that weather of her mother's skin had begun to glow a ... color. She watched as her mother's ... eyes ... and closed, ... A terrible ... and call flooded Noor's heart.

In an instant, Noor charged the ... creature. Screaming as she crossed the room, Noor raised her **arms until** her hands were extended horizontally toward the **creature** as though to push it. But really she had no plan. She was completely overtaken by pain **and concern** for her mother. She was certain her mother was dying in the creature's grasp, that she was being killed by it. Her only desire was to stop the creature from hurting her any further, even at her own expense.

So, it was a surprise to her when, at the moment she touched **the icy** shadow of the creature's exterior, she heard herself utter the **flame note** of the ... of Power. She didn't know why she had done so, but it was the note she had been taught to use when in need of defense. The tiny, wispy note created in a small coal of flame that **burned** without oil, a fuel, air, wood, or stone. She had learned to use it in the making of potions, often to heat the delicate fire

... Yet, ... they exist ... however, ... dead, ... bone-white wood ... time and termites ... gaping like a maw.

... clear ... in the hollow. ... the utter stillness, ... a sacred ... dread, and I whimpered at my edges. ...

... shadowy ... on the ground, ... a low growl, ... facets ... looking in deeper and deeper. **Soon,** Noor's mother was breathing regularly. Soon, she had even opened her eyes.

Noor cried out **with happiness and clutched** her mother in her arms. Noor sobbed with joy. Weakly, Noor's mother put her arms around her daughter and held her close in return, **whispering softly.** But Noor couldn't understand her mother's words, so Noor put her ear closer to her mother's mouth.

"What is it, mother," Noor whispered back. "What can I do," she asked.

"It was the end," Noor heard her mother say. But she did not understand what her mother meant.

"What?" she asked. "Whose end."

"The Americans'," she said. "The explosion. I still touched off pure hate." Then she smiled and closed her eyes.

Noor **said nothing,** she barely cared. She was just happy the Americans had gone, hopefully for good, and her mother was alive. **The night** grew late, but the two women were **too hurt and too weak** to do much of anything. They ignored the door that had been blown off its hinges, the broken furniture, the shattered glass of all of the windows and doors. Instead, leaning on each other as they walked, the pair made their way **to** the bedroom, where they each dropped into their respective bed, and fell into a deep and **dream-** less sleep.

It was many days before Noor or her mother could get

alive?"

"Partly, yes."

"Then,   ⬛   a wave of
          body.
        pleadingly   .

                              .
"B   hurt
                              ."

                              ,
driven by fear. "   "
                          .

"B   . "

                              ."

      ⬛
      away.   to sing,

          held
in ⬛⬛⬛⬛⬛⬛⬛⬛⬛⬛⬛⬛⬛⬛⬛⬛⬛⬛⬛⬛⬛⬛
                  .

                the scent of   ,
                        moonlight,
                              .
              ,   meadow.
                        .
                              . A
                an invisible rhythm,
                              ,

Noor sat beside the creature, patting and singing to
it, she saw its ██████████ calm and grow deeper. Noor
was **relieved** the creature seemed to relax some, for
she had no illusions about the situation. Examining
██████████ Noor thought that **death** was cer-
tain and **would come** soon. Although she believed she
couldn't save the animal, she felt that she could at
least ease its passing. Thus, she resolved to stay
with you **until** it was done.

With one hand on the creature's fur, Noor let
her other hand fall to her side. There, **it landed on
the mossy bank and began to alter.** Although not know-
ing why or how, she felt her fingers dig into the
damp earth beneath the mossy stones, where they began
to alternate. Suddenly she felt compelled to close
her eyes. In her **mind** she **saw roots emerge from under**
her fingernails and travel through the ground. Once
more, **the Song** of Power surrounded her, as it had
when she was **a child**, and, **mingling with** the song of
the trees, her spirit reached into **the earth, meeting**
the connection that had risen to answer her call. Then,
at the moment of contact, when **fungus and vegetable**
fingers met, Noor felt a wild path in her other hand.
The soil, **suddenly** loose and now, had lifted free
and other her, holding her hand in its mouth like
a mouth for the **liquid** in her veins to go into the
soil's womb. But, Noor felt no pain, no ache, to
tear from the clutch of the soil. Noor knew it was
not acting aggressively. As soon as the hand
opened into the soil, the soil released Noor's hand
and lay back down on the bank. There, again, with

"What is it?" Noor whispered, afraid to speak too loudly. But Noor was met with silence, heavy, like a wave swelling in the offing. The expression on Noor's mother's face remained stolid. Searching for some modicum of certainty, Noor noted the deep, familiar wrinkles at the corners of her mother's eyes and mouth. **The wrinkles held,** like stained furrows, an ancient collection of trial and change, and were juxtaposed on the smooth, impossibly white **mycelial** skin of her cheeks and forehead. Although her **expression** had not relaxed, it had not sharpened either. Her eyes, brilliant and dark, looked far into the cold, deep into the night. To restore warmth, Noor dared that Noor whispered she had feared Noor's absent son. In her own unease, Noor desired to repeat it.

"Mother, what...." However, before she could complete the sentence, the echo returned. Even softer now, the howling sent shivers down Noor's spine. So pained, so angry, **it seemed to never end.** Noor stood, fear and anxiety building uncontrollably through her blood, her eyes darting back and forth between the front door and her mother. Noor had **something** to call into to the village at that moment, **wild with** rage and terror, and to tear the two of them apart. But her mother's expression remained stolid. Noor could barely do that there, which was a comfort, but a deep **seriousness (or was it** sadness) had settled heavy on her **mother's jaw,** her head. With all her longing on the unbreakable, her breath to escape. But that wasn't so.

Finally, the scream stopped. Noor was

... the creature and ... .

"Mother, ... A... ...type," ... ...
asked, ... why ... ...
... ...,
... ..., ...
... ..., ...

"A... A...type is a ... of human ...," ...
... ..., "a ... ... of ... and ...
... ., ... of human ... , ..., ...,
... ..., ..., ..., ...
... ., ... A...type is a ... ... of any ...
of ...'s ... ...
of ... ...
... ."

... ... "... ... ...
... Before ... ..., ...
... ..."

"..., ... A...type, ...
... ...," ...'s ... ... "...
..., ... A...type ... ... of ...
... ..., ... to ...
... ..., ..., ...
... ..., a mirage, ..., ...
..., of what is, ...
... ... people ... ..., ...
... ...
... ..., ... cannot act on its own."

"But ... ...!" ... ...
... .

strategy to confront and destroy it. In any case, this seemed like the only course of action I could now reasonably take, given the situation. So, in essence, I hunkered down and waited, and, while I waited, I watched. Time and fate would have to come along to my side.

   .   .   .

that now passed since that first night-hunt in the forest, and little has changed. I have remained close enough to the village that I can easily keep an eye on it, but the villagers remain murderously frightened of me and the meaning of my presence. However, it seems that my strategy of strict nonviolence has at least reduced the number of attempts on my life.

In the first few weeks after the Archetype's arrival, the villagers, in the initial fervor and zeal to kill me, organized hunts every other day or so. But they always ended the same way: either the hunters never got close to me, which I always preferred, or I summarily withdrew and fled without harming anyone, hardly leaving a trace. This happened often enough that I think the hunters began to grow bored or frustrated with effort. Never getting close to one's quarry can have that effect. But, whatever the reason, the hunters soon reduced the number of hunts from one every other day, to one a week, then to one a month. But if they hadn't lost of me, for sometimes I would feel encroaching by stretching a later too close to the edge of the forest where I would overhear the gossip of some nearby

... a blankness ... bound by ... innocence ...

"... dead!" ... "... dead!" ... opened her eyes to find a young, ... woman ... inexplicably ... of her.

"... ." ... She was ... lost, ... happened. She looked around. It took a moment, but slowly the ... of the familiar ... the ... of the ... returned.

"... you would, but ... have a ... ," ... the woman, ... her ... , her hands trembling about her mouth. "... all of the dead ... were your fault. Oh, ...!"

"Death." ... repeated. ...

structure of her throat could not make such sounds —
was clear and close. It was **like** the song of **roots
whispering underground,** like the rolling of leaves in
wind, like flowers opening, or like mycelium spread-
ing and tangling in the hidden earth. Enraptured,
Noor listened and followed. But soon, as she found
the song, its beauty seeping just out of reach, she
became desperate to find its source. Suddenly, she
was walking in what seemed **like** the direction of the
emanations. Then, she was running. As she followed
it, she noted with surprise the power of her legs,
the strength of her body, the force of her heart.
Each step was sure and strong as she bounded between
stone and tree, jumping over ditch and stream.

     Thus, she went, deeper and farther, farther and
deeper, following the song into the forest, wanting
to sing with it, ●● ● ● ― ●. But the
song of the trees was always just beyond the reaching
of her ears, just outside the hearing of her tongue,
beckoning her to follow, her mother's song gone en-
tirely now. For kilometers, Noor chased it, plunging
onward again into the deep woods, hour after hour, los-
ing track of time, losing track of body, until it was
late at night, and she was still running. Soon, ex-
hausted by the duration of the effort, though still
driven to find the song's source, Noor slowed to a
jog, **then a walk.** Her feet heavy and aching with her
travel, her breath labored, Noor stopped, completely
exhausted. In a moment, darkness took her. Feeling
the soft grass of a meadow against her cheek and
hands, Noor fell asleep out in the open, the song of

... ..., ... attention ... ...
... ...

... ... I
... ...,
could see them, not on my body, not part of my body,
but like a series of lakes viewed from a ... ...
peak. ... ... the vast pool ... ... b ... ...,
... ... with ... . the ... ...
light of ... ... out with a ... ...
... ... explain. ... ... to pa... a... ...,
... ... and ..., a... ... ... to ...
..., ..., and ... the hellscape around me.
Then, there was a feeling of buoyancy. ... ...
... ..., ... and ...,
... to ..., ..., and ... ... a ...
... of ... pool. ... ..., ...
and cruelty collapsed ... ... and ..., ...
... within membranes of selfless ... .
..., ..., ... pulled ... ..., ...
... ... and movement, the transmutation ... ...
... ..., pulled ... ... like a child from ...
..., and ... ... dark.

... opened ... ..., ... the dust
... ... of ... ... Around ... ...
... of ... ... Ba... ... and
..., ... at ... with astonishment ... ...
... ... get too close, ... did ... ..., ...
... ... B... ... ..., ...
... . Weak and heavy with sorrow, ...
... to ... . one ... . B... ... ...
... ..., ... was getting low in the

o.o. In any case, the question was moot since there was nothing she could do to improve the situation. So she'd had to put the worry out of her mind and to pay attention to that she could sense. As the moment of the journey became familiar and repetitive, and the peace of her mind once more calmed and reliable, doubt could contort in the outcome that the Archetype was likely unable to mimic its surroundings with such overwhelming degrees of freedom. She and so felt confident, now that so many points had passed without it, that she could maintain her focus to get to her final hour.

Thus, hours time passed. Although doubt did not ever call to prove it and repel the corners and refrain from another attack, although the fear subsided to the near ability to see through any challenge the Archetype might use, she couldn't shake the dread of the almost certain return. Deep in her being, she knew that she and her other did not have the strength to repel the creature, let alone defeat it. This doubt was present on day one after the attack, but in the weeks that followed, it had aged at root, especially because of her mother's own demise, and it had become a part of her obsession. The creature would often be a constant presence. It could even appear while she slept, lurking in her head, and could at times haunt her night.

Also, look that while she was not going to permit that had happened her to one of an archetype look at here. Besides, she could not permit to go into the dark truth of her thoughts, and thus, she went to look that on her thoughts, and thus, she went to look night, look that had made her so

ness registered the coolness of the ground lingering
a few inches below the surface. It drew my attention
downward, and soon the mycelium answered my subcon-
scious call, rising up and surrounding my fingers. In
an instant, I knew the direction the Archetype, still
disguised as the black bear, had taken. I walked to
the spot where Deart and creature had entered the un-
derstory and located the tracks and scent. It would
be easy to follow, but I couldn't leave just then.

        Soon the **sun** was beginning to rise. I found a
shaded area behind a large boulder, protected by a
wild hedge of bramble. It was here that I began to
dig a grave for myself, for that part of me named
Nial. The work was hard, but as I (that is, all that
remained of me) scraped at the parched earth, some-
thing happened. Something dislodged, and I realized
that I was not just **digging a grave** for Nial, I was
also digging a grave **for** my **mother**. Like never be-
fore, visions of her death flooded my mind, and the
sadness and grief I never expressed found their way
to the light of my awareness. Again, I watched, as
though I were back in the cottage of my childhood, as
a similar mind and entity, **while the vines** welling
up from under my mother and from **inside her** while
the roots and runners, reaching out and wrapping
around her face and body, pulled her into the earth,
earth, drawing her back home. And as the **tears** began
again, I saw the face of the Archetype **curling** into a
grin and smile while a moment before the ground fell
away and it was taken as well.

        When **the grave was dug** I lowered Nial into the

...the unconscious slide into ...

But ... a wry smile ... despairing, ... ready to strike ... But ...

... But ... limited to ...

... elucidation ... But ...

-- her foraging trips to the town midden or the surrounding ███ were now done **in secret** -- Noor thought it was unlikely the woman would recognize her. So, Noor decided to lie.

"I am," she said, gathering as much authority in her **voice** as her scattered and uncertain mind would allow. Immediately, the woman fell to her knees and began to weep wildly. Through Noor, the woman spoke,

"I seek your aid," she said ███████████ "There is no where I can go. Please, help me. I seek your aid." Noor regarded the scene ███████████ yet another strange sight. Without the usual distrust, the supplicant had appeared, **begging for** mercy. Noor felt the woman's **earnestness**, and she grew less suspicious of the woman's motives. Reaching down, Noor put one hand on each of the woman's shoulders and raised her to her feet.

"Come in," she said smiling. "I will help you." Noor felt the **muscles in the** woman's shoulders go all, her eyes rising to meet Noor's. Slowly, the woman now freed her face from her **scarf** to show that she too was smiling, that she meant Noor no harm. To Noor's mind, the woman was surprisingly young, now showing the depth of her sorrow. Yet her face was red of skin and **swollen from endless weeping**. Noor saw, then the woman's youthful attempt at a smile, and a more tears to come, wet beneath the surface. "Come in," Noor said again, softening at the face of the woman's despair, and guiding her through the door of the ark.

to the woods. For a long moment, I listened and
watched. A light wind blew, and I put my nose to it,
breathing deeply, searching for signs of the bear or
the Archetype. I smelled neither. Both seemed to have
fled, or they had fled as one, I couldn't remember.
In either case, I was alone, and, for the moment, it
seemed, out of harm's way.

Satisfied with my safety, I turned my attention
to the feelings of grief and bewilderment I had expe-
rienced earlier. Still they stopped, but I did not
understand them. In the confused state of my battered
mind, I could not comprehend what had caused them.
But I thought the answer must be nearby. So gathering
my strength, and leaning against myself, I slowly
stood. Then, I walked, or staggered really, to the
opening of the tree, leaned on the threshold and
peered inside. In addition to the three human bodies
still lying where I left them, there was something
new. In the center of the cave, a shadowy lump of
tattered fur lay motionless and visible.

Immediately, I understood, and again I shat-
tered. I fell to the ground and wept and howled. I
tore at the earth and at my fur and ears. I ap-
proached the brink of insanity, peering into the hole
now had in the world wider and complete. But alive I
remained, a broken mass, hearing this voice speak the
entirety of my body as I crawled toward the birthplace,
lump of fur, closing the gate that as I approached.
For I could remember it now that he was no longer a
barrel of flavor, no longer an absent of my mind. Now
I could remember how to speak of self as a separate

tire. Then, as my body slowed, it would grab me in its tentacled arms and drain me. Afterwards, it would drain more and it would be one. I be would be trapped forever in a world of eternal dark and eternal pain.

Yet even at the edge of despair and defeat, I didn't give up. I continued to point and read, to sprint and parry, keeping the creature's attention from focusing on Noor. But as I read away from one its thrashing tentacles, my tired body was suddenly struck by another arm, and I crashed into Noor, who collapsed unconscious on the ground. A moment later, stunned as I was, another part of me was about in its relentless grasp.

Pain lit me up. I went along with it, and I went insane. I jerked and bit and thrashed and flailed. Noor left me, as I screamed and writhed and fought, as, wildly, I lashed out, desperate for the door, to read, desperate to get away.

Then, all at once, the pain was gone. Looking up I saw myself, still in the grip of the Archetype, my body torn and bleeding, my voice lost in the space, my throat battered. Disoriented and weak, I lay on the ground, in a corner of the cell, in the broken doorway. I was done. I couldn't even move. I waited for the end.

But, at the final moment, as the shadowy form that seemed to swell with immense pride, I saw something in its presence. It was Noor. She was out cold, and she was fading. As I gazed I read of the gloating creature, she began to walk toward me with slow

broken

fears of difference.

appearance

blooming from their ears.

such was

the great paradox of

interaction between

presence

and silence

"Yes what you think is wrong. I have felt it. I am not what you think you see, Witch. And I am not what you think you have seen."

"Yes, you are right," Noor's mother snapped back. "You are worse. Besides your hatred of life, besides your bitterness and bile, besides your jealousies and rage and your petty cruelties, you are stupid and arrogant," spoke Noor's mother, the power of her voice mounting.

"Ha!" the Archetype laughed. "Mortal language!"

"You are nothing!" shouted Noor's mother. "You are the shadow of what Evil beckons."

"Oh, I am not a shadow, Witch," the Archetype growled. Then, raising its voice, it continued, "I am both dead and death. I am both the ravaged and the ravager. And I am both the hunted and the hunter."

"Be gone!" commanded Noor's mother. Noor felt a burst of energy emerge from her mother's throat. But the spell was ineffectual. The creature remained in its chair, smiling. Noor was horrified. She had never seen her mother's spell fail before. Noor had never even considered its failure a possibility.

"I am beyond you," told her the creature, laughing. "There is nothing you can do. For I am not shadow. I am here, and I have come to be restored, and the abomination of this world be rectified. Bring me your daughter and I will show you."

"Bring you my daughter!" Noor's mother roared.

...wanted ... to **close** her eyes and lose herself into ... So close now, blankness ... the **bliss**, ... she ... yet something stopped her and ... urged to let her go. In fact, it seemed to hold her there, to keep her awake, ... some ... up to ... with. At first it had a vague sensation, a pear... ... with about the wall opposite ... of the tree. But the longer she listened the more it had ... Soon it had become **a nagging thought** ... Loor's mind. She couldn't quite put her finger on it, **but** it seemed to lead away from the grove, **to** pull her ... the opposite direction of the Loud of the tree, to ... and **prevent** the death of the tree.' Loud. But ... more that ... that there seemed to be pain in the thought, and sorrow, which irritated her. She didn't want to think about ... Wanted it would go away and leave her alone, she wanted both to do with it ... She didn't want to feel the hurt, the ... of ... from **its sadness**. Loor closed her eyes and tried to close it out.

But the nagging idea would not ... Eventually, Loor, ... finally found ... **the desire to disappear**, and ... the safety of its embrace and, thereby, her own. She tried to turn her attention on it and found that the tighter she would ... seemed to be ... from ... a point in the lower core ... beyond the line of her own trunk. She decided to investigate it and ... toward ... when she stood up that her body was still quite strong deep in the feeling of extreme ... love, ... when she began to lose it, her ... evolved.

village among the unsuspecting humans, and I let its
evil work against them unchallenged. Worst of all, I
let it repeat itself.

Before **I had completely departed** the cemetery,
I knelt in sorrow at the foot of one of the smallest
graves. Beside the larger mounds of earth, this one
seemed **pathetically** tiny, fragile even, and it broke
my heart. Without thinking, I put a hand on it, as
though to comfort the deceased infant which lay be-
low. But, as soon I did so, I was flooded with the
pain and **suffering** the poor infant also had been
forced to endure before the Archetype released her.
The agony was unbearable, unending, and horribly fa-
miliar, for I had experienced such suffering before.
I had seen the same asphyxiating darkness and had
felt the same sadistic tearing at my soul. I had been
brought to the same edge of death, the same moment of
escape, and then been denied it, again and again,
forced to return to my body and to endure the agony **of**
renewed affliction. With great effort, I pulled my
hand away, horrified by what I had found, by what I
had found again and had pushed out of my mind. In a
moment, I was gone from the place, fleeing as fast as
I could, running as much from the horror of the Ar-
chetype as from my failure to stop it.

The sun was beginning to rise as I arrived at
the small cave I had come to call home. Here, in-
side, on a bed of dried leaves and moss, I lay, quiet
and spent, alone in all sides. After the cemetery,
it felt good in my nature to lie down quiet and still,
wrapped in the folds of my own warmth. It came as

Trees loud in her ears.

.... to the .... of ...., her body ...., her mind ...., the .... all to the ..... of the ...., ..., ... of .... an opening in the trees in front of her. From the dark shadows in which she found herself, the .... was ...., and she squinted against the ..... in her eyes. ...., ... into .... saw that she was .... prone at the edge of a .... meadow .... with violet, orange, and .... Around the meadow was an .... grove of .... oak trees. ..... was awestruck. .... had .... trees so large or so .... old before. They stood .... of all ...., the .... and .... of oak and .... too old for .... saw ...... an undercurrent to the .... beauty of her surroundings. Something .... was also here, something .... and ....., ... in ...... sleep. Strangely, though, ... she ...., ... also was ...... They were frightening: .... of ..... and ....., the ...... of oak and ....., the ...., ... of .... they had fallen. They .... A... the ...... and wildflowers was the ..... of the ...., the ..... to ..... to ...., so close to ...., beckoning still.

..... say back down on the soft grass and .... to the trees .... to .... Bathed in their melody, ... felt .... sleepy. All the

unutterably grateful. She thought she might start

to calm herself. She took some deep breaths, wiped

her eyes and whispered a kind of mantra that she asked

her. In a moment or two, she had again gained control

of her emotions, her mind now reaching for the

still terribly frightened.

"Mother, please, listen to me, what is that,"

she pleaded. In time, her mother moved her eyes

from the door and looked at Moor almost kindly.

"A hat," she said, her voice flat and matter of

fact. "That is a hat."

"What. A hat." Moor asked incredulously, the

light dancing in her mossy hair. Over the years, she

had seen and heard plenty of men. None of them had

ever roused her, remotely like that, not even the

ones who seemed the angriest and the most dangerous.

In fact, they did not seem capable of that so much a

"Yes, a hat," repeated her mother, her eyes re-

turning to their vigil of the door. "But a lost a

one."

"What do you mean, 'lost a one,'" asked Moor.

"The ones dressed are ones, and a monster."

Quickly, Moor's mother stood up. She began to

the doorway, pulled her body away, and turned again

her, Moor followed suit.

hands to her temples and singing **a few notes** of the Song of Power **softly** to herself as her mother used to do when she was young and scared, Noor was able to regain her self-control. She recognized the trajectory of her mind and focused her consciousness on the stream of debilitating thoughts and feelings that were coursing through her. Almost ██████████ the full force of the fear and self-doubt began to diminish. Soon she was able to think more clearly. Soon she was able to act, which she needed to. She then lit the candle on her nightstand with **a flame** summoned to tip of her index finger.

Having that handled herself, Noor's attention now turned to the living room where mother and Archetype faced each other. Closing her eyes and singing the song again, but this time using inflections of voice she had come to know as her mother's, Noor was able to establish a telepathic conduit to her mother's mind, to see out her mother's eyes.

In front of her, stood what indeed appeared to be a man, but one made haggard by time and neglect. With a tangled beard, **wiry,** white hair, deep, scar-like wrinkles, hunched back **and tattered** clothes covering an emaciated body, Noor's first impression of the Archetype was to wonder how it had generated so much force to shake the house as it had done. However, when she looked into its eyes, she understood that there was more to the creature than its physical appearance, for its gaze was deep, focused, almost incomprehensibly deep, focusing in on a... It grasped at her in a motion and one that seemed to overwhelm and menace-

...able to sleep, ...pped the rest of that night
thinking about my situation, and how best to proceed.
From what I have told you, you will know I do
...ot...e...tion the village, ...ave decided that I would
never sleep close to the village again. I learned that
too ...ly. I also learned that I could never again
...timate the people of the village nor the Archetype
again.

Once more, I reflected on the comedy of the
Archetype's motion. It was clearly that it had behaved to motivate and organize a... no quick...ity. But,
as a result, I was able to see the true nature of the
... situation. Now, the Archetype's next step seemed
obvious. If it hadn't already, it would tell the ...
...ders about the presence of ... ...on it had ...eared on
the way to the village, and it would blame me for
them. Of course, the people of the village, thinking
it had ... who spoke to them, would believe the A...
...etype. But the villagers would think they had
out... the Archetype's story or ... to more
...tes of abomination them... over the ... ...ty
days.

...still for it seemed to be at quite
a disadvantage and there was nothing I could do to
stop the villagers from going to those dens of ... .
There was no time to ...dge what was done, so I had to
deal with the aftermath. How could I ... people to
forget the ... created by the Archetype, an
...e la...y ... - the possibility of a national ...ou...
... with the others now seemed impossible. Realistically, I, at least, had ... ...ould to refrain from

...harming any of the humans in my first encounters with them. Limited as it was, this strategy of nonviolence would have to be **the foundation of** my response to the Archetype's lies. I simply could not give any person in the village **actual evidence** ███ █ ██ ██ ██ █ of good-

███████ ███ I then had to hope for some opportunity
███ ███ ███ engage the people of the village in a
███ ███ ███ then the nature of **my character**

For now, however, I decided to rest as I needed to. The events of the last few days had utterly exhausted me, and I knew I would need as much strength and stamina **as possible** to manage the current **situation**. So, for the next few days, I hid in the cave, and slept. It felt good, but what really helped me was not sleep, **but** the **grief** I felt for Mial. Each night, as the forest **grew quiet and the** moon **rose over** the trees, I felt the weakness in my mind and **my body** that had resulted from his death. It left a hole in me that was almost intolerable, and I had to be careful to keep it free of rage. For vengeance is what I **wanted**, bloody revenge. I wanted to invade the village and attack the Archetype before it could regain more of its strength. However, I knew this was ███ **a lost cause**. The Archetype had already surrounded itself with enough protection to make a direct assault impossible. Yet, over time, even if only for a few days, I felt the hole settle, and adjust, let myself reinvigorate without Mial, and that I could be stronger, perhaps not as strong, but certainly whole, and alive. This way, I could learn more of the Archetype's plan, and perhaps find a...

...free herself from the grip of the Archetype's voice, from the weight of the gaze, her mind turned to darker, more imaginary behaviour. Having lost control of her imagination, Noor was **helpless** against an onslaught of perverted **visions**. With a mixture of horror and grim desire, she saw herself tightly gripping on her own hair, tearing at her hair, scratching at her eyes. She watched herself enacting all visions **of obscene** bodily self-mutilation permeated her mind, sickening her, yet bringing her to the edge of action.

But in an instant, the dream dropped away. Noor sat left in the silence of her crowded cell, horrified by the dark turns of her **imagination**. Her, she had to let go. She had not left her mother's mind, and before long, she watched as her mother, still **guarded and unreachable, open** her eyes to reveal the Archetype still sitting, just as it had been, in the immense hall in front of her, with the same remaining mask and cold, featureless black eyes probing her mother's mind.

"There is nothing I can do **to help** you with that," Noor's mother said wearily.

"You are wrong," said the Archetype, with a the wisdom. "**There is so much you can do.** You think you know me, but you do not. You think you know what I am, but you are wrong."

"Do not doubt, Creature, that I know you more than you would like, for I have seen you before," replied Noor's mother, her agitation becoming obvious, her anger rising, strength returning to her voice.

... on and her hand. Infinitely beautiful, ... there ... ... mind, louder and louder, beauty upon beauty, ... the pain was overwhelmed by the ... tones of ... the music . ... Moon's obliteration ... longer, and ... ... seemed to enter every cell of her body, ... to resonate ... ... the music reached its highest pitch, ... upon the ... tones of the ... ... upon infinite brilliance, ... however ... until ... had fallen ... to sleep.

Thus, Moon ... a process of ... motion and transfer, ... not so much something else, ... Day by day, ... from ... and ... the ... to the Song of the ..., with a kind of ... to that approached the infinite potential of ... ... It was like a death that ... ... the crushing ... of ... that ... ... world, ... formed ... of ... ...

...so eager to

the air was ■ muddled with

what had occurred.

, things began to happen . a viable target, a unified

In front of me

via the corridor on both sides of . the bank o

for harvest. It seemed plausible that this apathy might also extend to their regard of the Archetype, a superstition had grown about it. Nevertheless, I could see that the villagers had tried to save themselves, at least for a time. From my initial wandering, I knew the village cemetery was situated close to town. The burial ground I now found myself in was an afterthought, likely out here to create distance between the dead and the living in an effort to slow the spread of the plague or whatever it was they thought was attacking them. Of course, that failed, as did their efforts to protect me, and now they were resigned to death, perhaps even welcoming it, having lost so much already.

I knew there was little to gain from going to the village that night. Instead, I needed to think. I needed to figure out a way to fight and defeat the monster, or, at least, to expose it to the villagers and to show them the real threat in their midst. Perhaps there was still strength enough among them to drive it out. Yet, as I began to withdraw from the grim scene of the children's cemetery, I felt hopeless. I had arrogantly and foolishly permitted myself to inflate my own importance, thereby overlooking the vulnerability of the townspeople. I was overconcerned with my own safety and, as a result, fell blind to the deaths of who-know-how-many people or how many children. In short, I had failed. I had failed utterly. I was the one, the only one, with knowledge of the Archetype, with knowledge of its abilities, and I did nothing to stop it. I let it live in the unblinking, a statue in the infinite ___, ___ ___ ___ ___ ___ ___ ___ ___ ___ ___. B__ ___ ___ ___ ___ ___. A ___ ___ ___ ___ ___ ___ ___, ___ ___ the dense canopy. ___ ___ ___ ___ ___, ___ ___ ___ ___. ___, ___ ___, ___ stood and stood. ___ , ___ ___ ___, ___ ___ ___, ___ ___ ___ ___, ___ ___ ___ ___ ___. ___ ___ ___ ___, ___ ___ ___ ___ ___ ___ ___, ___ ___ ___ ___ ___ ___ ___ ___ ___ ___. ___ ___ ___ ___ ___ ___ ___ ___ ___ ___ ___ ___, ___. ___ ___ ___ ___ ___ ___, ___ ___ ___ ___ ___ ___ ___, something beyond knowing ___ ___ ___ ___, ███████████████████████ ___ ___ ___ ___ ___ ___ and ___.

Thus, ██ entered ██ vagueness, ___ ___ ___ ___, ___ ___ ___ ___ ___ into Day, ___ ___ ___ ___ ___, ___ ___ ___ ___ ___, before the birth of thought ___ ___ ___ ___ ___ ___. ___, ___ ___ ___ ___ ___ ___ ___ ___ ___, ___ ___, ___ ___ ___, a ghost among trees, ___ ___ ___ ___ ___ ___ ___ ___, ___ ___ ___ ___ ___ ___. ___ ___ ___ ___ ___ ___ ___ ___ ___ ___ Day ___ ___ Day, ___ ___ ___ ___ ___, ___ ___ ___ ___, ___ ___ ___ ___, ___ ___ ___ ___ ___ ___ ___ ___ ___ ___ ___ ___ ___ ___ ___ ___, ___ ___ hardening ___ ___ ___ into bark, ___ ___ ___ ___ ___ ___ ___ ___. ___, ___ ___ ___ ___ ___ ___ ___ ___ ___ ___.

ter, I decided, what they said. The important thing
was that none were killed, and **none were** injured be-
yond any **accidental** scrapes or bruises.

    So, I escaped. I ran into the safety of the
deep woods, this time unconcerned about staying close
to the village. I just needed to get away from the
farmers **before something terrible happened,** and I
succeeded. Before long -- my pace so much faster than
theirs -- I was alone in the darkness, panting in the
pools of moonlight that gathered in the silent forest
many kilometers from the village. Nevertheless, for a
short while, the farmers tried to continue the pur-
suit. It was ridiculous of course they never got close
again. They must have been confused by how easily
they had **kept up** earlier in **the night** but now were
falling so **hopelessly behind** I **just wasn't** taking
any chances.

    I ran at top speed until, first, the torches
were no longer **visible,** and I continued until I was
far **enough** away, I couldn't hear the voices of the
men nor the barking of their dogs. Still, I didn't
stop there. Onward, I continued, slowing after their
sounds became more and more indistinct. Only then did a
feel that I had put enough distance between us, that
if the door could technically reach me here, I was
sure that I was simply too deep into the forest for
the humans' comfort. They would turn around, fearful
of more than just me, long before they got close.

    Thus, I managed to evade capture and avoid a di-
rect confrontation with the people of this land on
the first night that I had come **to live near them.**

comfort. But, before long, I began to weep. I wept
for all the lives I had let slip from my protection,
and I wept for the narrowness of my vision. I wept
for the limitations of my power, and for the weakness
of my will. I wept for my cowardice, and I swore neo
to never be afraid again. I wept for the suffering
that I had allowed to be perpetrated on an innocent
and unknowing species. I knew what I had to do, and I
would do it before noon again occurred. Then, as I
drew myself in as tightly as I could, I tried to
sleep.

.   .   .

I woke to a massive wave of indistinct agony.
It filled my mind like a sound, like a scream, like
scream upon scream, heralded in total horror. My
thoughts thick with it, I rose from my pallet in a
panic and ran out the mouth of the cave without know-
ing where I was headed.

But once outside, I stopped. The sudden rush
into bright daylight had blinded me, and I squinted
and rubbed my eyes, waiting for them to adjust as a
sharp pain coursed out to them.

In the distance, people were screaming. The
cries came from the direction of the village, horri-
ble cries, cries of death and pain. I ran toward
them, my chest with sudden rage, and with a grim de-
termination to end this thing.

Soon, I saw coming a crowd, a ragged
and drained, scattered on the forest floor. They were
the poorest of people, men and women and children;

separate the a⸮⸮⸮⸮⸮ o⸮ ⸮e⸮ ⸮ea⸮⸮ from the ⸮⸮⸮⸮al
distortions caused by ⸮⸮a⸮ ⸮⸮⸮⸮⸮ ⸮⸮ ⸮⸮⸮⸮⸮⸮⸮⸮⸮ a⸮ ⸮⸮⸮
A⸮⸮⸮⸮⸮⸮⸮' ⸮⸮⸮⸮⸮⸮ ⸮⸮ ⸮⸮⸮⸮ ⸮a⸮, ⸮⸮⸮ ⸮⸮⸮a⸮ ⸮⸮ ⸮⸮⸮⸮⸮⸮
⸮⸮⸮ ⸮⸮⸮⸮⸮⸮⸮, ⸮⸮ ⸮⸮⸮⸮⸮⸮⸮ ⸮⸮⸮ ⸮⸮a⸮⸮, ⸮⸮ ⸮⸮⸮⸮a⸮ ⸮⸮⸮ ⸮⸮⸮
⸮⸮⸮⸮⸮⸮⸮⸮⸮. ⸮⸮⸮⸮ ⸮⸮⸮⸮⸮ ⸮⸮a⸮ ⸮⸮⸮⸮⸮ a⸮⸮ ⸮⸮⸮⸮a⸮⸮, ⸮⸮⸮
⸮⸮⸮⸮ ⸮⸮⸮ erosion o⸮ ⸮⸮⸮ ⸮⸮⸮⸮ ⸮a⸮⸮⸮ ⸮⸮⸮⸮⸮ ● self.
⸮⸮⸮⸮⸮⸮⸮⸮⸮ ⸮⸮⸮ ⸮⸮⸮⸮ so lost and detached ⸮⸮⸮ ⸮⸮⸮⸮⸮⸮
⸮⸮⸮ ⸮⸮⸮⸮⸮ already ⸮⸮ floating ⸮⸮ a universe o⸮ ⸮⸮⸮⸮⸮
⸮⸮⸮⸮⸮⸮⸮, ⸮⸮⸮ ⸮⸮⸮⸮ ⸮⸮ ⸮⸮⸮⸮⸮⸮ ⸮⸮⸮ ⸮⸮⸮, ⸮⸮⸮ ⸮⸮⸮⸮, a⸮ ⸮⸮⸮
⸮⸮⸮⸮ ⸮, a⸮⸮⸮a⸮⸮ in ⸮⸮⸮ ⸮⸮⸮⸮⸮⸮⸮⸮ possession ⸮⸮⸮⸮

⸮⸮⸮ ⸮⸮⸮⸮⸮ ⸮⸮ ⸮⸮⸮⸮⸮⸮⸮⸮ ⸮⸮ ⸮⸮⸮⸮⸮⸮ ⸮⸮⸮ ⸮⸮⸮⸮
⸮⸮⸮⸮ ⸮⸮⸮ ⸮⸮⸮⸮⸮⸮. ⸮⸮ ⸮⸮⸮⸮⸮⸮, ⸮⸮⸮ ⸮a⸮ a⸮⸮⸮a⸮⸮⸮ ⸮⸮ ⸮⸮⸮
⸮⸮⸮⸮⸮⸮⸮, a⸮⸮ ⸮⸮⸮ ⸮⸮⸮⸮⸮⸮ ⸮⸮ ⸮⸮⸮ ⸮⸮⸮⸮⸮⸮. ⸮⸮ ⸮a⸮⸮ ⸮⸮⸮
⸮⸮⸮⸮ ⸮⸮a⸮ a⸮⸮ ⸮⸮⸮a⸮⸮⸮⸮, a⸮⸮ ⸮⸮⸮ ⸮⸮ ⸮⸮⸮ ⸮⸮⸮ ⸮a⸮⸮ ⸮⸮⸮
⸮⸮⸮⸮⸮⸮ ⸮⸮ ⸮⸮⸮ ⸮⸮⸮⸮ ⸮a⸮⸮ ⸮⸮ ⸮⸮⸮, ⸮⸮⸮⸮⸮⸮a⸮⸮⸮ ⸮⸮⸮⸮⸮ ⸮⸮
⸮⸮⸮⸮⸮⸮ ⸮a⸮ ⸮⸮ ⸮⸮⸮⸮. ⸮⸮⸮ ⸮⸮⸮ ⸮⸮⸮ a ⸮⸮⸮⸮⸮⸮⸮.
⸮⸮⸮⸮⸮ ⸮⸮⸮⸮ ⸮⸮⸮⸮⸮ ⸮⸮ ⸮⸮⸮⸮ ⸮⸮⸮ ⸮⸮⸮⸮⸮⸮'⸮ ⸮⸮ ⸮⸮⸮⸮⸮ a⸮⸮.
⸮⸮⸮⸮⸮⸮⸮, ⸮⸮⸮⸮ ⸮a⸮ a⸮⸮a⸮⸮ ⸮⸮⸮⸮⸮⸮⸮⸮⸮⸮ ⸮a⸮⸮⸮⸮ a⸮ a⸮⸮.
⸮⸮⸮ a ⸮⸮⸮⸮⸮ a⸮⸮ a ⸮a⸮⸮ a⸮⸮⸮⸮ ⸮⸮⸮ a⸮⸮a⸮⸮, ⸮⸮⸮⸮'⸮ ⸮⸮⸮⸮⸮
⸮⸮ ⸮a⸮ ⸮⸮⸮⸮⸮ ⸮⸮⸮⸮ a⸮⸮⸮ ⸮⸮ ⸮⸮⸮a⸮ a⸮⸮⸮⸮⸮ ⸮⸮ ⸮⸮⸮ ⸮⸮⸮ ⸮⸮
⸮⸮⸮ a⸮ a ⸮⸮⸮⸮. B⸮⸮ ⸮⸮⸮⸮ of all ⸮a⸮ ⸮⸮⸮ ⸮⸮⸮ ⸮⸮⸮⸮
⸮⸮a⸮⸮⸮⸮⸮ ⸮⸮ ⸮⸮⸮ ⸮⸮⸮⸮⸮⸮'⸮ ⸮a⸮⸮⸮. ⸮⸮⸮⸮ ⸮⸮⸮ ⸮⸮⸮⸮⸮⸮'⸮
⸮⸮⸮⸮⸮ a⸮ ⸮⸮⸮ ⸮⸮a⸮ ⸮⸮⸮ ⸮⸮ ⸮⸮a⸮⸮, ⸮⸮⸮⸮⸮ ⸮a⸮ ⸮⸮⸮⸮⸮ a
⸮⸮⸮⸮ a⸮a⸮⸮⸮⸮ ⸮⸮⸮ A⸮⸮⸮⸮⸮⸮⸮. B⸮⸮ ⸮⸮⸮⸮⸮ ⸮a⸮ a⸮⸮⸮ ⸮⸮⸮⸮
⸮⸮ ⸮⸮⸮⸮ that ⸮⸮⸮⸮ ⸮⸮⸮⸮ ⸮⸮ ⸮⸮ ⸮a⸮⸮⸮ ⸮⸮⸮ mother's
⸮⸮ ⸮⸮⸮⸮⸮. B⸮⸮⸮⸮⸮ ⸮⸮⸮⸮ ⸮⸮ ⸮⸮⸮ ⸮⸮a⸮ ⸮⸮ ⸮⸮⸮⸮⸮ ⸮⸮ ⸮⸮⸮
⸮⸮⸮ ⸮⸮⸮⸮' ⸮⸮⸮⸮, ⸮⸮⸮ ⸮⸮⸮⸮ ⸮⸮⸮⸮ ⸮a⸮⸮ a⸮⸮ hope

B⸮⸮ ⸮⸮⸮⸮⸮ ⸮a⸮ a ⸮⸮⸮⸮⸮⸮ ⸮⸮ ⸮⸮⸮ ⸮⸮ ⸮⸮⸮⸮ ⸮a⸮ a
⸮⸮a⸮ ⸮⸮a⸮⸮ and ⸮a⸮ a⸮⸮⸮⸮ ⸮⸮⸮⸮ a ⸮⸮⸮⸮⸮ ⸮⸮ ⸮⸮⸮ ⸮⸮⸮⸮
⸮⸮. A⸮ ⸮⸮⸮⸮⸮ ⸮⸮⸮⸮⸮⸮ ⸮⸮⸮⸮, ⸮⸮⸮ ⸮⸮⸮⸮⸮⸮ a⸮⸮⸮⸮ ⸮⸮⸮ ⸮ ⸮⸮
⸮⸮⸮ ⸮⸮⸮⸮⸮⸮ ⸮⸮, ⸮⸮⸮⸮ ⸮⸮⸮⸮ preemptively annoyed ⸮⸮ ⸮⸮⸮

..........., ..., I began to whimper. ...., ..., ..., ... Shallow gullies remained where .... Ago.. ... . landscape .... A...... ... . faded ... ..., ..., ... disturbingly ... ., ... Whatever happened ... ...

... ... the earth ... ... had occurred, ... B..... ... ., ... I accompanied and, ..., ..., ... I began to search. B..... ... ferns ... ., ... human footprints ... ..., ..., ... a low tangle of vines, ... broken and rotting ... .. a simple .... cart, ...

alive.

I watched with horror and pain as Noor stepped into the open and approached the cabin, desperate to see her mother again. It was terrible, but she had lost all caution, lost all sense of danger. Within a moment she had mounted the steps to the porch and was knocking at the door. Then, she waited. Noor heard the gritty sound of feet shuffling on dirty floor-boards, of footsteps moving closer. From my position, I saw the movement of shadows beneath the door. Finally, it opened.

In the pale light of the cabin, the two recognizable women regarded each other, skin stained with lichens, vines growing from their hair. Noor exploded into a paroxysm of sorrow and joy. She began trembling, instinctively raising her hands to cover her gaping mouth. She was weeping. "Oh, Mother. Oh, Mother," Noor repeated again and again. "Oh, Mother, you're here! You're still here!"

Tears formed in her mother's eyes, though she said nothing. A loving smile grew on her lips, but she made no sound. Instead, Noor's mother reached out gently and held Noor's shoulders. Her hands moved along Noor's arms until they reached Noor's hands, which she took softly in her own. Stepping backward, she led Noor into the cabin.

It was bare. No furniture, no fire, nothing. Just a dim light that glowed from nowhere. But Noor was too overwhelmed, too moved to notice. Her eyes were fixed on her mother, who was pulling gently,

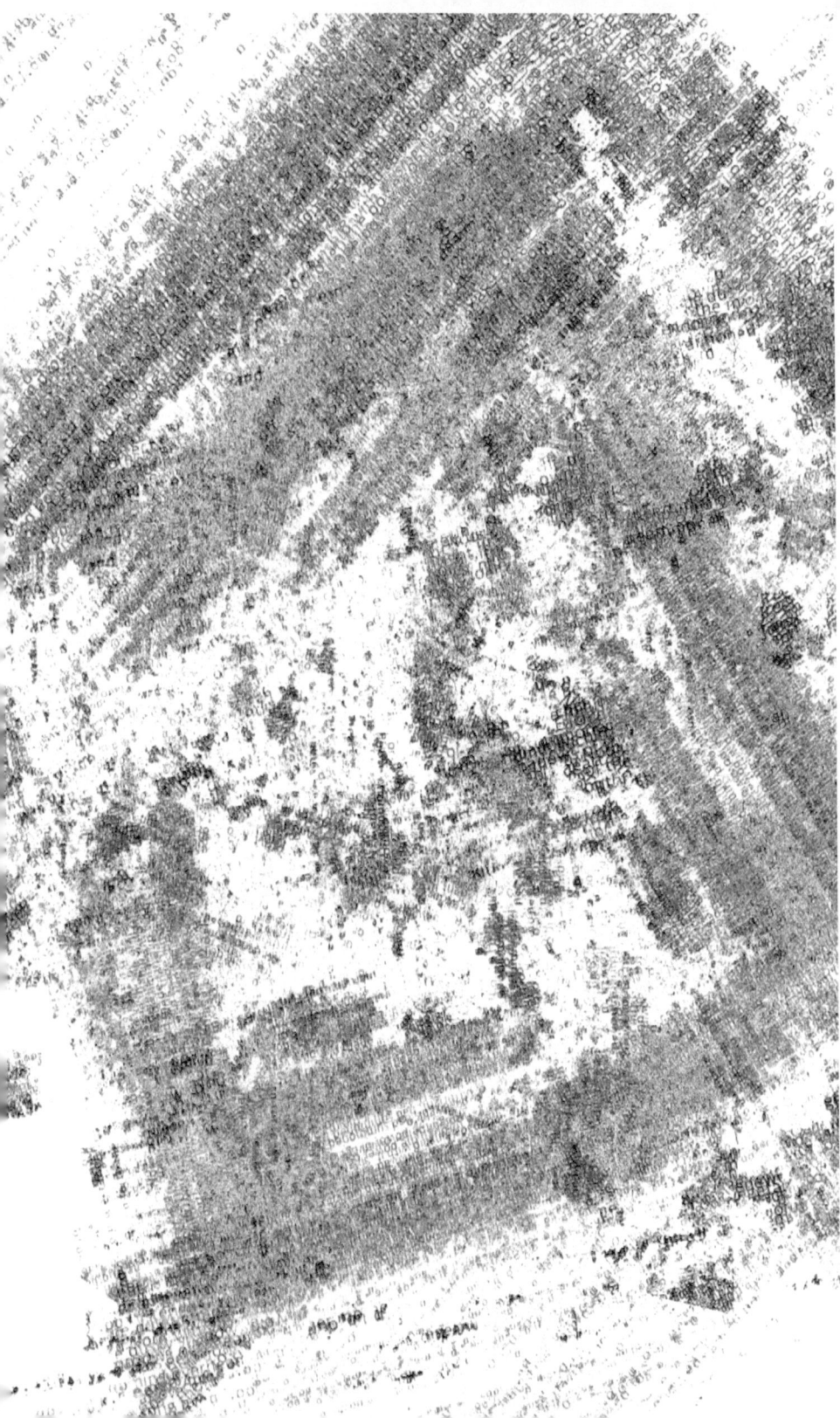

to defeat it, likely, I now knew, at the cost of my
life.

.   .   .   .

Night fell, but I continued. Despite the pitch-
black darkness, despite feelings of terrible expo-
sure, despite the sounds of unnatural horror that
seemed to surround me, I pressed on. The presence of
the Archetype had faded to a dim light in my mind,
and its tracks were scentless now that it had forsak-
en earthly disguise. But I continued, hour after
hour, chasing **the** tatters of the Archetype's move-
ments, **pursuing** the **fragments of** its escape that lin-
gered in my mind. Thus, I followed, darkness thicken-
ing, until all at once, the presence was gone, and I
was forced to stop.

Blindness weighed on me. I groped for direc-
tion, but found only silent stone, mute tree, and
voiceless earth. I tripped over fear and disorienta-
tion, stumbled on rock and **indecision.** I fell, hope-
less and **trembling,** and waited **in the dark.** Huddled
and scared. At any moment, I was certain I would be
taken, helpless as I was. At any moment, I knew the
final blow would come, my body shivering and tense
with dire anticipation. I closed my eyes. But noth-
ing happened. Darkness thickened; time stopped. I be-
came nothing in an infinite void.

Then, out of nowhere, it began. Softly, at
first, at the edge of perception, a sound underlying
my thoughts. Then, louder, almost inaudible, but grow-
ing in volume. A faint melody. Familiar. Nearly

of ... terror like a sludge ... my mind. Something terrible had happened here. I knew it.

Carefully, I mounted a low ridge that over-looked the parched and pitted earth of a remote forest road. Although I now had some relief from guilt to survey the area, I also appointed simultaneously to lookout points, 30 meters to the north and 30 meters to the south of the ridge, fearful of being flanked or surrounded. Then, I turned my attention in all directions at once. This was a dangerous part of the forest, so near at the edge of the realm of men. It was a liminal area, too close to human settlements for most protective creatures of the forest to be comfortable, but far enough that evil had the opportunity to take root unnoticed. So, I knew I had to be cautious for many reasons. But the air was clear, and everything was quiet, still. Once in position, I was too.

Then, I waited. And I waited. The minutes passed, and nothing stirred. It was strange. There was no activity in the forest. No creatures moved around in the undergrowth. No birds sang in the canopy. The stillness was claustrophobic, as though even the wind had been banished from the spot. Yet ordinarily nothing seemed amiss. Beyond the abnormal quiet, the beauty of the forest, no strange glints, sounds, or smells presented themselves. Instead, sunlight streamed prettily through the branches of the forest's dense foliage as it would on any usual summer day.

This wasn't what I had expected. In some ways,

the slow ethereal and methodical swirling of the
heavens.

slow ethereal and methodical
heavens.

..., ... the peeling façade ...

..., ... of the same deep forest. ... ... the loathing ... strangeness, ... that grew ...

... with sorrow ... ... faces twisted in ... ... windows. ...

small vials of

elegant,

combustion.

the door

now

infused

by

matter.

the door

for two hours,

notes emerged

and light

So oblivious, so weak,

I renewed

my own mind, and resolved to keep

the sprung traps.

like so much trash.

it was not for the best.

stalemate. Since I could not get close to town or to speak with the farmers, I consulted the imperial **network** often, looking for indications of the **Archetype's** movements, hints to its plan. Yet, as far as I could tell, the Archetype remained steadfastly **hunkered** in the village. It was difficult for me to **continue** to deny this visually as the farmers had built several **makeshift** lookout towers at the corners of the village, equipped with watch dogs stationed at their bases. This made it even hard to get near the village unnoticed.

Sometimes, however, late at night, when everyone, including the dogs, was asleep, I was able to creep up to the edge of town. There, I'd see the darkened windows of the villagers' homes and the quiet and empty street that ran through the village center. If the moon were full, or near full, and the **sky** clear, I'd be able to see from one end of the village to the other, and I would marvel at the peacefulness of the human settlement. Everything was still, dark and sleepy, and I envied the sense of comfort and safety I felt looking at the farmers' homes.

But, below this peaceful facade rested the **human** vulnerability. The villagers had no idea what tiger lay coiled in their midst, what manner of beast stalked them in the shadows of their bedrooms. Even if I couldn't determine the whereabouts of the Archetype, I could sense it, lingering somewhere in the village. If it so counted, there was nothing the townsfolk could do to protect themselves against

Although ███ had █████ to ███ ██████ and to ████ ███████, ██ ██ █████ ██████ to █████ ███ ███████, ███████ ████ ██ ███ █████. ████ ███████ ██ to ████ ██████ ████ ██████, and ███ ████ ██ ███ forced ██████ to ████ ███ transgressive ███████ ████ ██████ ███████ ██ ████████████ ███ █████ beauty ██ ███ ████ ██ ███ ████. ███ ██████ ███ █████, ████ ████ ██████ ████ █ ███ ████ ████ ███ ████ ██ ██████. ████ ████████ ████ ███ ██████, ███ ███ ██████ ██ ██████. ███, █████ ████ a few steps away ████ ███ █████, ███ ████ ██ ███ ████ ██ ███ ████ ██████ ██████ ██ ██████ ████, ██████ ██ ██████████, ███ ██████ ██ ██ ████ ██████████. ████ ██████, ███ ████████████ ███ █ ████ ██████████. ███ ██████ ███████ █ ██ ██ to ██ away into the soporific ████████ ██ ███ ████, ███ █████ ██ ███ ████ forever ██ ███ ███████ █████, ██ ████████ ██ ████████. ███ ████ ████, ███ ████ roots stirring in her toes, vines dancing in her hands. █ ███ ████ ████ ██████ ████ ███ █ ███ ██ ███ ██ ████ ██ ████.

But ███ ███ █████ ████ ██ ████, █████ ██ ██ ███ ███ ███ ████ ██ ███ ███ ██ ███ ████, ███, ██ ███ ███ █████ ██ ██ ████ ███████ ███████ ███████ ██████ ███ ███ █████, █████ ████████ ███ ████ ███ ███ ████ ██ ████. As ███ ████ ██████ ██ ███ █████'█ ███ , ███ ███ ████ ███ ████ ████ ██████ ███ ██ █████. ███████, ██ ███ ████ █████, ███ ████ ██ ███ ███ ████ ██████ ██████. ██ ███ ████ ████ █ ███ ██ ████ ███ ██████, ███ █████ ████. ███ █ ██ ██ ███ ██ the face of mortal vulnerability. ██████ ██, ███ ██████ ██ ███ ███ ██████ ████████. █████ ██, ███ ███ ██████ ████ ████

useless, ...

... that is, ...

... hazardous, ... I rested ... fed up with ... the open, ... the ... young ... the ground ... moaning and writhing in pain, ... But seeing no one, ...

farmers as they worked — I was always hoping for some
news of the Archetype, its actions or its schemes —
they would raise the alarm. Soon enough a group of
armed farmers with dogs would appear and chase me in-
to the woods.

For the most part, however, they had stopped
hunting in groups all together. I concluded that they
felt safe ▇▇▇ I ▇▇ left their minds — I was
sure the Archetype saw to that — or they at least
came **to accept** the **futility** of direct attack; that,
or, despite the Archetype's efforts, **the intensity of**
fear within the settlement had faded. However, they
had not given up entirely. In place of the hunts, the
farmers now filled the forest with traps and snares.
In my daily rounds, I now came across pit traps,
filled with sharpened logs and covered with brush, a
variety of deadfall traps, ground snares and spring
snares as well as leg hold traps and **conibears**.

Like the hunts, these always failed, **obvious as**
they were, because the villagers did not understand
me, and **everything** reeked of human. They could not
think of me as anything but an animal perversion, a
single-minded monster, which meant their techniques
never significantly evolved. Perhaps, it was the Ar-
chetype's fault. Perhaps the Archetype, for whatever
reason, could not convince the farmers of the extent
of my intelligence. Or perhaps, the Archetype, overly
confident in his own sense of intellectual superiori-
ty, couldn't see beyond my ruse either.

Whatever the case, the farmers soon abandoned
the **snares** and traps, too, not only because they were

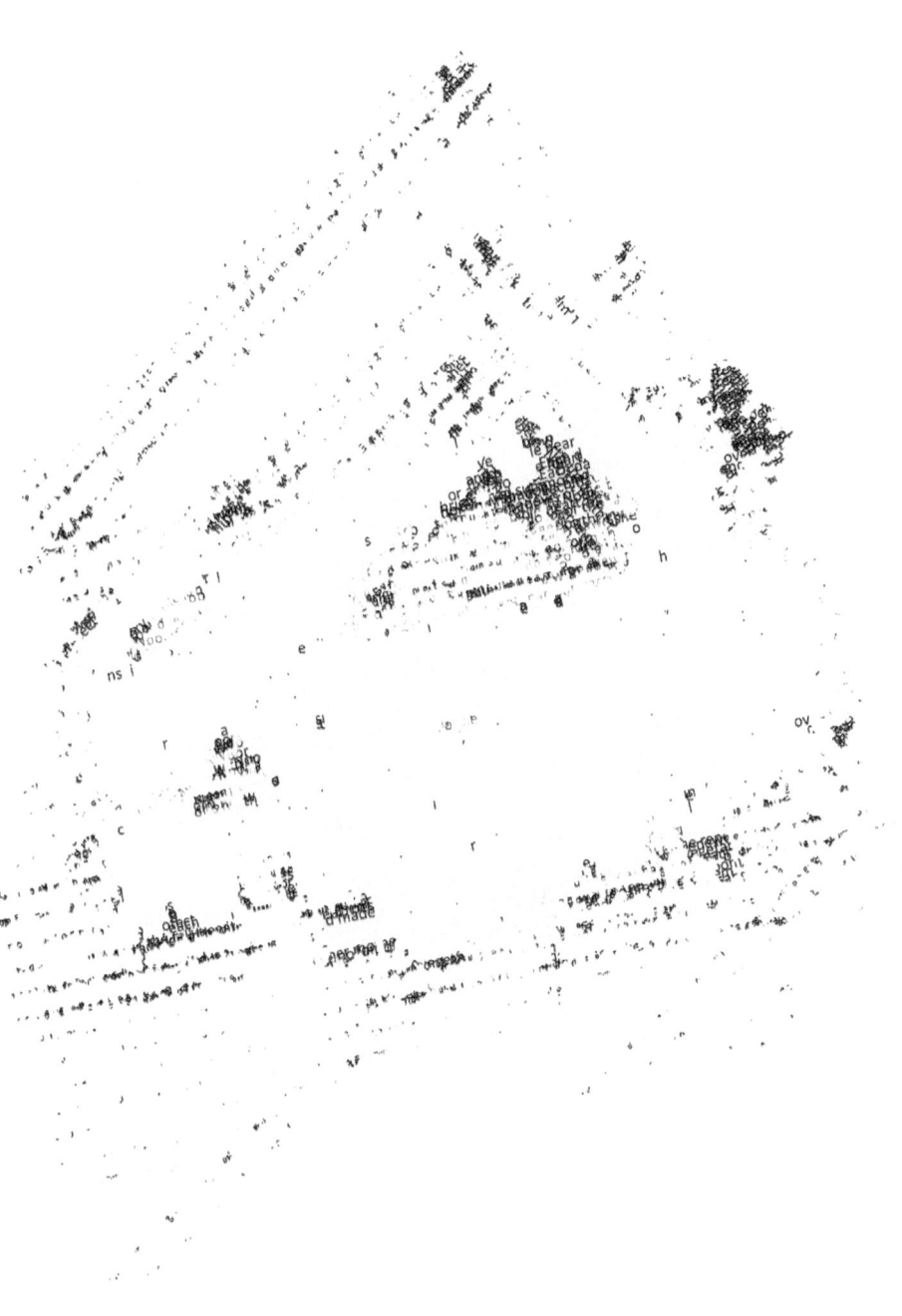

time, while the song remained for the most part un-bearably beautiful, she began to learn its melody and rhythm, and she began to understand its movements. This greater understanding in turn led to feelings that the song was leading her to something, that she was following it somewhere. This gave her comfort, although she was powerless to resist it.

In any case, she was able to remain in the world for longer periods of time, for which she was grateful. On occasion, at moments when the pain was faintest and the song softest, Noor remembered her former life. She recalled the Archetype and her mother's death, would feel the sorrow and grief, but they seemed far away. There seemed to be some kind of protective distance between her current self and the self that experienced the memories of her now seemingly distant past. Yet, she knew the memories to be her own, and she knew them to be important. It was just that they could not destroy her now, could not dominate her, would not form points of detrimental fixation, limiting her ability to learn, act, or grow. Noor was again able to understand her situation, the likelihood of approaching danger, and the need to find a new path.

One bright morning, Noor awoke to the song of the trees and early morning air around her. She couldn't understand why, but, without the usual pain, the notes of the song burned more brilliantly, more vividly, than they had ever done before. And it a language that lingered on the brink of comprehension, the melody, although she could not reproduce it, the

of felled [illegible] now [illegible] the landscape and a [illegible] **quiet** [illegible]. Forest creatures are not [illegible] [illegible], and most will flee the environs of people, aware of the danger [illegible]. But the Archetype's tracks continued, pressing further into the land of men, so I, [illegible]

Eventually, I came to a long, high hill. Although the tracks of the Archetype went directly up and likely over it, [illegible] catch the scent of anything that might be on the other side. I feared the Archetype might have also realized this and used the occasion to get a lead. So, [illegible] to spread myself to the hill, to have a look around before [illegible] being my entire body, or, ultimately, [illegible] the idea. If something happened at the top, I wouldn't be able to respond in time to save myself. Plus, now I was wasting precious time. [illegible] at the Archetype before it reached the safety of [illegible], I had to move quickly, which meant I couldn't waste time reconnoitering or looking for a way around, even [illegible]

So up I went, moving as quietly and as quickly as I could. In minutes, I had reached the top without incident. From there, I looked down the backside of the hill and at that [illegible] the westernmost of the woods. Two hundred meters from the base of the hill, the trees gave way to [illegible] ones [illegible] **green** in the afternoon sun, but indistinct through the trees. My eyes, so used to the **shadows** of

altogether too much credit and, by extension, inflat-
ing my own importance. Wasn't it just as likely that
the Archetype had just gotten **bored or hungry** and was
now **gorging** itself **on** the people of the town. Wasn't
it just as possible that the available need for per-
adiation had overcome its **restraint** in some ways,
and now it was **running amuck.** And wasn't it possible
that the healing of men, exposed to the will of the
Archetype for so long ago, may have been twisted to
evil by something they never saw.

Whatever the case, I needed more information
before I could decide on a suitable course of action,
and getting closer to the village would be key. Since
the villagers now appeared unconcerned with my pres-
ence, I might be able to do just that. But, before
setting out, I thought it best to wait for darkness.
Also, because I generally stayed to the east of the
village where the forest was thickest, I felt that,
if there were a trap, they would be expecting me from
that direction. So, I circled around the village and
approached from the north. That night, there was a
waning crescent moon, a day or two from the new, but
the sky was clear, and my visibility was good. Thus,
I came to the northern edge of the forest in the deep
of the night, or the early morning without incident.

Initially, I avoided the northern part of the
village, mainly because there was a lot of open .
Most of the farmers' fields were situated there, and
a great expanse of open land lay between the edge
of the woods and the start of the town. However,
though, the trailer lay quiet, as I had **hoped** and

... to conjure ... their skin ... vivid as ... Boo ... weakness ...

... the unrelenting ... temptations to ... marrow ... like parasites ... leech-sorrow ... extirpations.

... laughed even less. ...

the moment and **to her** understanding of herself as healer. she could feel the pain of the **cry's bearer** as her own, and now wanted to help.

Her pace quickened, and, to her relief, walking soon became easier. With each stride, she felt less tired, **less sleepy.** Soon the cry was clearly the cry of **a wounded creature,** the desperate **reaching** of a spirit at the brink of death. When Moor's full strength had returned, the grove now behind her, she quickened her pace even further, running now, running toward the cry, her spirit reaching in response to the call.

Driven by the need to **succor** an afflicted animal, Moor followed the cry into the deep shadows of the forest. In a spot away from but still near enough to **the grove,** the song of the Trees remained loud in her ears, Moor came upon a crook in a mountain stream. There she found a wolf lying **bloodied and half-conscious** on a mossy bank of stones. Moor approached slowly, cautiously, and knelt beside it. The wolf appeared to be in pain, its chest heaving as it struggled for breath. **Looking closer,** Moor saw a **large gash on** the wolf's side, then areas where the wolf's fur had been burned away leaving discolored patches of skin like her own. Moor's heart bled for **the dying creature. Reaching out** a tentative or voluntary hand, Moor found herself patting the animal gently, feeling notes of the song of Power resonating in **her throat.**

But the wolf did not respond to Moor's touch. **It didn't move** or seem to be aware. Even still, as

I didn't ⸻ ⸻ to do. Like ⸻ ⸻, ⸻ ⸻ the creature via any means available to me. ⸻

⸻ So, in an instant, I decided that is what I would do. Yes, I would ⸻.

⸻ headlong and snarling. ⸻

wildflowers and plantains.

invariably body throbbed with skin torn or the loss of home, do nothing but endure her eyes, braced against the torment. joy returned. writhing on the ground of disorientation,

It was **a grotesque** and frightening sound, like the bellow of a wounded cow beset by a pack of hungry wolves, and the shudder bolt of it had caused Moor to close her cloak tightly around her waist. Bent over, pale and feral, Moor heard death in the cry. And anger. All of it frightened her, but especially that latter sentiment. Although she was already at a ripe linked within, Moor was still young, having just passed the threshold of adulthood, and there was much of the world she had yet to **encounter** in life, her interactions with the world beyond the respectable walls of her home had been limited, especially of late, to forays into the woods to forage herbs, weeds, fungi, and other ingredients. Prior to that, Moor passed through a brief period of curiosity, venturing more to the village on several occasions, in defiance of her mother's warnings. When these excursions did go as well as she had fantasized, she soon abandoned them for the relative safety and quiet of the forest. Now, Moor watched her mother for clues on how to react. How serious was this situation? What was that sound anyway? Is it something she should fear or was she overreacting?

Moor saw that her mother had also stopped working. She had been preparing a resin from the dried flowers of the wild boar vine, a pile of withered petals on one side of her workbench and a small pot growing that **of black ellipsoid** pods on the other. Now, her hand rested not only on the workbench, a boar vine flower clutched in her right hand. She did not look at Moor but kept her **gaze** fixed on the front door. She seemed to be coiling part of.

But what of this

. whatever that means?

it had

to think

of the being that was

panic

called it a man, but so far, not man-like at all.

the forest, outlined against the brightness. The openness, or the exposure it implied, frightened me. Far, looking ahead, what I took of the Antelope, though I knew I would not be exactly know what it looked like, since it had taken a new human form. In any case, I saw no humans and I feared I was too late.

But I could smell them, or, at least, one of them. A strong odor of men emanated from the field below and rose up the hill to enter my lungs. I hoped it was the Antelope. Perhaps, I wasn't too late after all. Perhaps I could halt it before it reached safely among the oxen and larger numbers of people. Perhaps I could catch it before it got away.

I sprinted down the hillside to the forest's edge and peered around the open landscape. I saw I was too late, for in the field a group of men had already gathered. They stood about 100 meters from me, clustered around one man-headed man who looked to have been badly beaten. Even still, he was talking and gesticulating wildly while the group of farmers listened. Upon seeing me at the edge of the woods, the man suddenly stared wide-eyed and a look of terror spread across his face. Without saying another word, he slowly raised his hand and pointed at me. Then he let out a frightened cry.

The group of farmers turned and looked. When they saw me, fear also spread over their faces, then halted. A moment later the first stone landed with a thud on the earth at my feet. Then more came, then a hail of stones hitting the trees and around me from

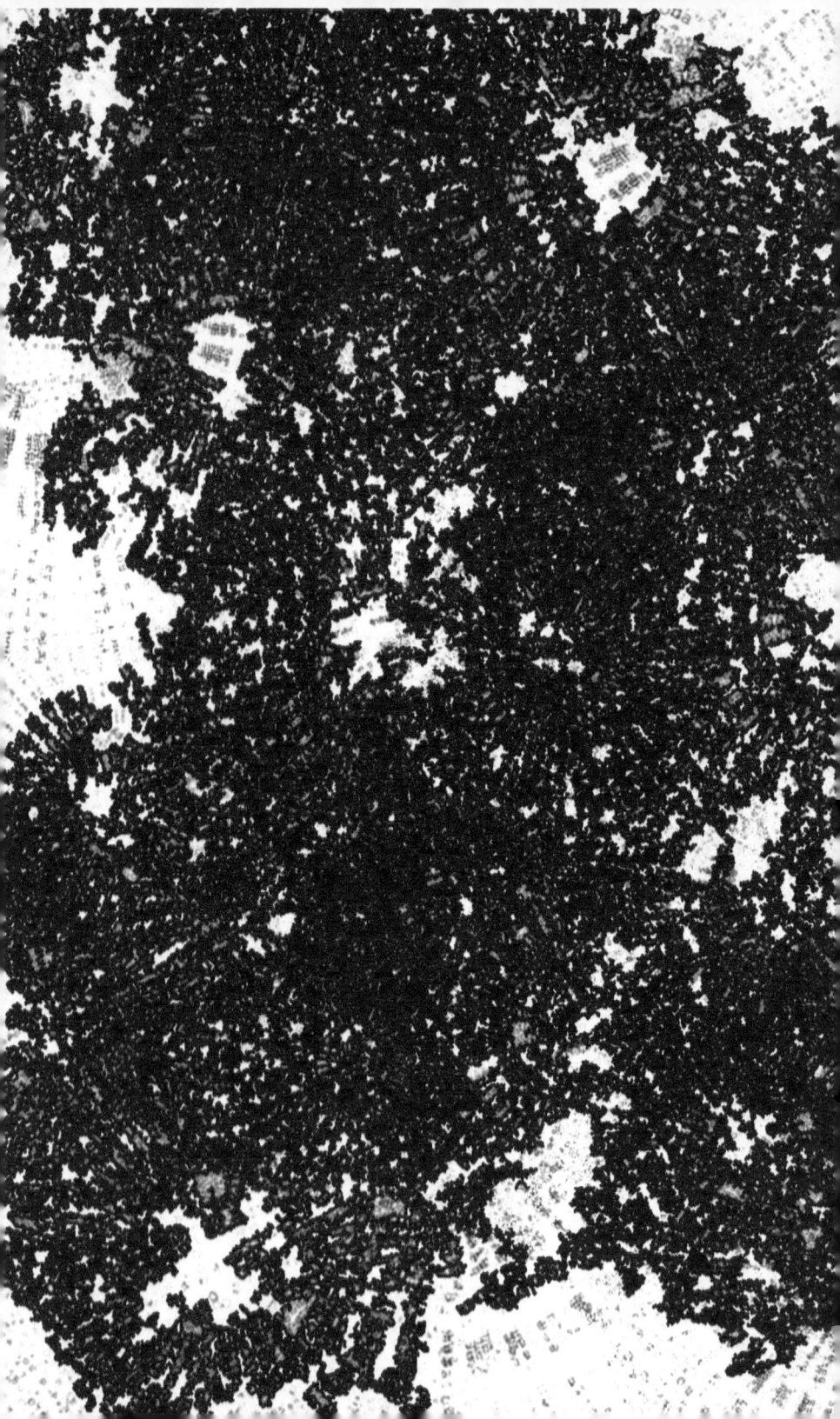

...to ransack...

...amusement, ...:

"..." ...

... to writhe ... like a parasite, to infect, to infest.

"..." ... to keep quiet. ...

"Death," ...

In the shuttered and cramped dark ... to endure ... to get away, ...

of that day, Noor recalled how she and her mother worked in silence, in awe of what had occurred. Intermittent waves of **unbearable beauty** washed over the young witch, and she often had to take time alone until the intensity of the feelings had passed. Noor's mother never objected or questioned her, giving Noor the space she needed to become herself. That night, exhausted by the emotional rigors of the day, Noor fell asleep quickly and easily, feeling for the first time in her life the profound connection of her being in the world.

Now, sitting in **a crook of roots** at the base of an Oak tree, Noor felt **horribly alone**. Any sensations of oneness, with nature, with her **mother**, with herself were gone. In their place were **vague** dread and an underlying but pervasive sense of distance **and** disconnection. Noor's mind was **cloudy** with it, and thinking was difficult. It reminded her of now, the first morning after the transcendence, a question had filled her mind. She recalled how it nagged her all day, wheedling away at her **memories of wholeness, like a virus of doubt,** causing pain. Eventually, unable to hold it in any longer, she turned to her mother and asked timidly:

"Mother, are there others." Noor's mother, also had hunched over the base of a large bell plant, digging at the roots, stopped and stood. She looked at Noor curiously.

"Others." she repeated.

"Yes, other witches. Are there other witches

Nevertheless, in general, the farmers kept up a well-tempered pursuit. Despite my **antics**, the does always seemed to come back into line, and they, soon enough, the group would be close behind again. No outward fear. I had no desire to meet there was in conflict. I felt no **anger** toward them, placed as they were, **and** I wasn't concerned that they would harm me. Quite **the opposite**. I would slaughter them if I wished, picking one off at time, pulling each into the dark with a horrifying scream, until in terror the remaining men fled back to the safety of the village. But I do not kill innocent creatures, nor for fun, and I do not kill for fun or sport.

Yet their persistence was unrelenting. Hour after hour, they chased me through the forest, zig-zagging this way and that, but always pressing me to the west. Slowly, though I did not know it, I was helping them in their plan. Not only did I notice them in their slow but steady westward movement, tracking obliquely toward the snare they had laid for me, but my directions seemed to conjure the idea of a snare. Eventually, we had run over the same ground from so many different directions so many times that I could not tell by odor where the threats and does were or in what direction they were heading. If they had to rely on sound, which had nearly failed me, all the others were silent.

Within the remainder **of the river's bend**, and close to the edge of the woods on the bank, another group of men had hidden themselves in **the brush**. There they waited with drawn bows as I was slowly

Thankfully, I was able to stop that trajectory of that thought. Rather, an overwhelming ████ re-vulsion stopped it. With everyone's eyes in my direction, I tried to hide my struggle, to hide my murderous hunger and my resistance to it; I tried to hide the truth of my situation. Perhaps, I was even trying to hide it from myself. But I couldn't. With a sudden shock, I knew what I was becoming, or had become, which meant I knew I could not trust my decisions any longer. I had to get away, for the safety of my friends and for my own safety, I had to get away from the town and get away too.

Without another word, I gathered myself and ran in the direction of the Archetype's retreat. The path was then enough in my mind, as was my goal, but there then was the reason for my haste. Reality, I just wanted to get away from the farmers, from the temptation to murder and to feed. I was afraid of the loss of these lands that had led into and blood. So, once in the woods, once out of sight of the village, and too far to be tempted by easy slaughter, I collapsed into a pile and wept. I wept for that which I had and for the evil within me. I wept for the loss of innocence, for the loss, the world.

But I could not weep for long. I knew who I had to become, and I had to trust myself to do a certain thing. So, I got to my feet, and I stood. Once more, I started to run, instinctively, my body spread out ready, speed along the ground and into the Archetype, its power and surety merging into me. Once more, I searched, on way or another, for some end and

... ... I was on a road that led to ... ...
... ... Bodies ... ...
... ...
... ..., the bodies of ... ..., ...
... ..., ... The
... ... trying to murder
... ... To ... ... death ... ...
... ...

... ... of the village ... ...
the dead. ... ...
... ...
..., to weave and jump ... ...
But ... ... village, approaching ... ...
... ..., in the bright sunlight ... ...
... ...
... ... hydra-like ...
... ... a tattered piece of cloth caught on the
heel of a muddy boot. ... ...
... ..., ...
... ...
... ... They were all that was left ... ...
... ... And ...
... ..., ..., ...
..., ..., gorging on their
souls. ... ...
... ..., ...
... ...

... ... physical ... ...
... ... Archetype, ...
... ... the shadowy ... ... beast ... ...
... ... hopeless. ... ...

closed eyes, the wolf lay on its side, **seemingly** un-
conscious, beckoning Moon to pet it.

As she did so, running her hand through the
wolf's fur in damp streaks, while her other hand
twisted among the mycelium of ow, Moon suddenly felt
as though she was no longer sitting on the bank of
the stream. Instead, she felt as if she were floating
in nothingness. It was an **instantaneous** change and
one that startled her. Afraid that she was falling or
losing consciousness, Moon opened her eyes and looked
around. There was **no forest and no stream**. The song
of the trees was gone, and the wolf **no longer** lay be-
side her. Trying to look down at herself, she did not
even seem to have **a body**. No pain coursed through her
hand, and she could not feel **the reach of** her fin-
gers underground. Rather, she seemed to be in a **form-
less space, not dark, not light, and without tempera-
ture. The surroundings** seemed to hum gently and, al-
though there was nothing distinctive to note, there
was a sense of vibrating, with colored movement all
around.

Moon was not frightened. There was nothing
threatening about the experience, however strange it
seemed to be. In fact, she felt a sense of wholeness
she had missed since **fleeing** the cottage. For the
first time since her mother's death, she felt safe,
calm. There was something that tied to her here,
something protected her, though she could not tell
fully what it was. Then, as she basked in the glow of
the glade, an **emotion**, or more, one more than one,
more tender, more generous, washed over her. The

...I was ... How, ... of ... to ... own body. ... the boy ...

..., returned to ... a ...

..., ... wonder. ...

..., I watched ..., limping ...

... shadows, ...

... safe in the company of ...

... failure, ...

... Things seemed ...

Young Lucy's cottage did not look like much. In fact, from the rutted dirt of the country road that ran before it, most passersby, if they noticed at all, thought it was just another humble structure of **wild mosses**, rotten wood **and** fallen leaves, blown there by the elements at the dark foot of a vast forest. But truth be told, no one could tell it, nor were they in need. Only the desperate could see the faint stream of **smoke** rising from the clay-covered chimney on the house's overgrown roof. Only **the wretched** could discern the shadow of windows curtained under mossy eaves. Only the afflicted could detect the **outline of** a door hidden amid the peat and bramble façade.

Of course, none of this was accidental. Lucy's mother, an ancient being with wine-white hair and dirt on her skin, knew what dangers surrounded her and her daughter. She knew the greatest threats did not come from the forest but from the nearby village three kilometers down the **dusty** road and from the farmhouses on the village outskirts. Although the forest was indeed filled with darkness and danger, it came no **hatred** like the hearts of men and women. Like the hearts of humans, it carried no dangerous fear of that it did not understand. **The forest demanded** no respect, but men and women must be regarded with mortal awe and fear.

To protect them, Lucy's mother, using the magic of her own blood, had summoned forth **the forest's** greatness and made kinship with it. Binding through the power of her **own vegetable heart** the grey roots, root and stem, root and leaf, persuading them to

...breath ... filled her lungs. Noor ... ... from the ... of it. But soon, Noor ... a ... deeply, and for a long moment she allowed the forest's dark air to ... her body and to wash over her still. ... she didn't hesitate for long. She didn't dare. Pushing herself up, Noor ran with new energy toward the impenetrable black of the woods, ... to the safety of the ancient trees. But once inside, she ... lost. Afraid of death, afraid of the ... ..., afraid of the villagers, but ... ... afraid of ... ..., Noor ... ... From darkness into darkness Noor ... deeper and deeper into the forest, the ... of the ... ... fading into the distance and the ... of the ... ... growing dim, ..., she did not stop. No ... ... to, on she ran, deeper and deeper, ... she did not know where she was, until she was utterly lost in the ... ... of the wild woods, until the ... ... of the trees grew so ... ... , they blotted out the sky.

So ... ..., Noor lay on a bed of ... ..., ... to the sound of her breath ... ... It seemed to be the only thing left in the world, the sound of her breath. coming and going, coming and going, ..., ... paused, ... her breathing ... again. She, she began to hear it, the sound of Power, though faint, ..., ..., the sound of Power, though dimmed, ..., ..., ... the dark. Slowly, ... of her ... ... power

... the ... Creature wide, ... close to the air. For whatever reason, the Antelope seemed to be heading toward a ... had fallen ... alarm on the western part of the road. ...

... to unspeakable ... the Antelope was born.

But after a few **hours** of ... , I began to detect another scent in the air. Above the trail of the wounded deer, I ... a separate current of blood, ... It was ... and fresh, like the deer's trail, and the strength of it worried me. ...

... , **brutally pungent**, ... Here, ... before, I **waited and watched**. ...

"Correct. It did. Which means it was **not** an Ar- chetype that **attacked** us. At least, not in the usual sense" **But** then she paused. Leaning back into the bed, Noor's mother was suddenly **deep in** thought as she considered **the implications of** what she had just said.

"Mother, **what is** it." Noor asked.

"I don't know," she replied, keeping her eyes fixed on the ceiling. "It was so much like an Arche- type, but **so different.** It sounded just like an Ar- chetype and behaved like one, but then it could also feed. It could take life directly from the body of a victim and use it to increase its **power.**"

"Is that what it was doing, feeding?"

"Yes, Noor, **it was.**"

"And these **splotches** are like death scars?"

"Yes, part **of** you had been taken. Those are the original marks of the loss."

"I remember, when I was looking out of your eyes, I had a vision," Noor said. "There was **a mob** with mother, led by the Archetype **in human form.** But then it changed. It grabbed me with its snake-like arm and dragged me into the darkness. It **strangled me.**"

"It was eating you, Noor. You would have died had I not been able to loose you out of my mind."

"I see."

"**And I'm sorry for that,**" Noor's mother com- forted.

and then to die, by my doing. I saw the danger lurking in the thought.

certainty in weakened refuge It likely knew I would not follow it into

The stumps

the woman's feelings had no anger in them. Though she was left wondering about her sudden suspiciousness, **the absence of** anger ultimately left her feeling compassion for the woman.

Moon Moo: pushed the foliage aside way, opening **a path** to the house. She listened as the woman approached, her **weeping** growing **in volume.** Before long there was a tentative knock at the door. Moon rose, then faltered. A smothering fear suddenly washed over her; **memories of** the Archetype's attack flooded her awareness. She suddenly found it impossible **breath.** In an instant, all the pain of the attack had returned. She again felt the pain **ripped from** her body, soul of self, organ by organ, thought by **thought.** She wanted to scream, to run, to get away, to disappear.

Overwhelmed by the flashback, Moon found it impossible to concentrate. Her surroundings spun and grew vague. Soon she was **on the brink of** unconsciousness. Grateful for release, Moon tried let go. The pain of memory was too excruciating, and the dread even worse. Without resistance, Moon allowed herself to sink deep into the darkness, hoping to be overtaken by the eternal **blankness** of death. Sinking in pain she go, she faded. But at the moment of final release, at the edge of escape, Moon, ready to be gone, to give up, to end this thing forever, remained. Heartbroken, she opened her eyes. There, she still stood, in the middle of the cottage, facing the front door, hearing the soft sobs of the woman outside, then another round of **tentative knocking.** Moon took a deep breath.

...so turn so that it was sometimes difficult to sleep at night. Too often, Noor found herself still awake at sunrise, sitting by the fire, listening to the **fading** dark. Humming softly to herself, Noor remained in a kind of **trance,** her attention extending to the surrounding area. All night, she had been listening for the ███ ▪ ▪ ▪ approaching Archetype, terrified it would again escape her notice. Thankfully, it never came. In its **absence,** Noor allowed herself to find **comfort in the** sounds of the night creatures of the forest, though often strange and unsettling, themselves. Even the **shrieks** of hunting or hunted beast were welcomed in so far as they were unequivocally identifiable to Noor's enchanted ear. Besides, something inside her told that she and the creatures were now joined by death bonder, which meant it would not creep up on her unseen again.

Nevertheless, there was always that moment between hearing a sound and naming it which caused great anxiety and trepidation. For also ever-present in the back of Noor's mind, there was **the question of** whether the Archetype could disguise or cloak itself as something anther. Since it could look and sound like a man, she wondered if it could also appear in other forms, as a forest creature perhaps, like a wolf or deer, or some other such benign presentation. If it could, she wondered if she would be able to see it through the disguise before it was too late, and the creature was upon her. However, since the Archetype was, as her mother had explained, a **conglomeration** of human negative emotions, she doubted it would take **the form of anything** other than something human

of me and behind. Suddenly, a group of farmers with
pitchforks and scythes charged, screaming, intent on
killing me. But I did not want to fight them. I had
no desire to harm those misguided creatures manipu-
lated as they were. But there would be no opportunity
to reason with them. Even under the best of circum-
stances my distributed form would have horrified
them. So there was nothing to do but run. I was too
late. The Archetype had reached safety and was now
working its poison into the hearts of men once again.
I retreated into the shadows, climbing the hill and
descending, easily outpacing the farmers' pursuit and,
I'm sure, half-hearted, pursuit. Soon, I was far from
the field, far from the smell of humanity, heartbro-
ken, but determined to fight as I could.

All that night, they hunted me. Men and torch-
es, dogs and wagons, a group of fifty men and at many
dogs attempted to track me down, tried to corner me to
the river that flowed on the western edge of the vil-
lage. As I could discover, the river made a large
peninsula like the mouth of a snare. They tried to
corner me into it and around me. They might have suc-
ceeded, too, had I not been stronger and smarter than
them, had they known me at all.

But really, it was just my own stupid fault. I
was too casual about the hunt, and I underestimated
the animals' abilities. I began with the dogs track-
ing me to where I lay in a well-concealed nook made
of a collapsed stone wall. I had decided to rest
there because I wanted to remain near the village and

...her eyes. ...she ...looked ...to her
...mother who was asleep in the next room. But her mother
...did not reply. At first, Noor assumed that she was
just sleeping deeply, ...the ...result of the
A...per's **draining** attack, but, ...the bad that
...and her mother had still not awakened, Noor felt
a ...deep dread.

...in the bad and forgetting about her age,
Noor approached the door to the bedroom and cautious-
ly opened it. "Mother," she whispered into the dark-
ness of the room. But again, there was no answer,
though she could now sense something there, something
in the room with her mother, standing with her in
the dark. With a flicker of ...hope, Noor lit the
candle on her nightstand and turned.

Before her, Noor's mother lay motionless in
bed. But it did not look like Noor's mother. Instead,
she was transformed, or, more accurately, in the pro-
cess of transforming. Noor watched as **vines** crawled
from her mother's mouth and roots grew out her ears.
Her eyes, no longer with a...spread across as she...
...in, **the candle's dim** light, Noor saw her now
sly..., **piercing** her mother's **wizened eyes** and
...up around her skull. Instantly, Noor knew her
mother was dead. In her heart, she recognized the
place. Her mother, the life force **around the house,**
was returning to its roots.

Looking up from her door, Noor saw a with-
...a gently tan with brown stains on her door and
hands, standing in the corner of the room. He no...

out bottom. She searched for food, also for the dis-
traction, but was then demolished by the memories.
Yet, food she still found, a sizable troop of short
caps in the damp crook of a fallen oak. So, Moor sat
and tried to eat. Fighting tears, it was all she
could do to swallow, even though the food did her
good. With each mouthful, she felt strength and ener-
gy return to her body; she felt her vision grow
sharper, her mind more alert. But the memories still
came, so distant as dreams, devastating as storms,
spurred by the interwoven metaphors of heart, mind
and matter.

"Mother," she heard herself say in a child's
voice, "are we mushrooms."

"No," her mother replied directly, stilling a
laugh. "We are not mushrooms."

"What are we then?"

"Well, we're witches, of course."

"What are witches," Moor continued after a
pause.

"Witches are born of the light of the full moon
held in the heart-fiber of the Mother."

"I am in your heart-fiber."

"Yes, Moor. As I was held in the heart-fiber of
my mother, you are held in mine. One day you will
hold your child in yours."

"But why do the humans call me mushroom and
throw stones at me."

... ... so many I thought ... ... of the ... ...

... ... of ... ... they ... ... to ... ...

... ... they turned ... ...

... ...

... ... the silent ground beside them, ...

... ...,

useless as the leaflitter they fell upon. ... kept

... ...

... ... reasons, ...

... ... the

... ... ready ... ...

... ... I ... ... The ... ...

... ..., still wearing the skin of ... ...

... ...

... ...

... ... broken. ... ...

... ... gaze ... ...

... ... wrapped in it, ...

... ...

... ...

... ... neck and face.

... ... smoke and glow ... ...

... ...

... ...

... ...

... I couldn't let that happen. Not again. ...

... ...

..., ..., ...

... ..., ...

... ...

... ..., ...

side. But I needed to know more. So, keeping an eye on the flames on the ground, I began to look for additional markings around the tree, searching for tracks or anything else that might have been left behind. In concentric circles beginning 1 meter from the tree's base, I expanded outward until I reached a distance of 10 meters from the trunk. Finding nothing, I returned to provide additional guard support to my front.

Once in place, I began to examine the interior of the cave further. I pointed to a thick and coiled the largest of the bodies, which, in the dim light of the hollow, looked to be a man. With a sudden jerk, the body raised its left arm and slammed it down on a small cloud of dust rising quickly from the floor. In an instant, I was falling backward through myself, while my rear came forward, reaching at the body. But nothing more occurred. The body lay motionless again among the others, and the dust settled.

Soon, I had reached my objective. I crouched and waited. But as the minutes passed, the bodies displayed no further signs of life and remained unresponsive to further prodding. So, I entered the hollow, and guarded the entrance. I approached the body, and with my nose low to the ground, I sniffed. Indeed, the largest body and the one that had moved was that of a man. The other two seemed to be the body of a small woman and the body of a child. Who, I wondered, took me, and I knelt beside them.

They were naked, and strange, and certainly

to change. The sky, at first almost blinding pale, began to darken. Soon it was night, then darker than night, and Noor watched a line of light continue to wind her through the darkness. The lights became too thick to follow, and the dark grey electric light and gathered. The **gnarled** hands of men and women stretched Noor's mind; bared **teeth** mouthing with fury and a shadowy tableau of **jerking in firelight** clawed her thoughts. So many faces, so much twisted, they seemed to strangle Noor. Then cold arms of shadow reached from the dark, gripping Noor's **throat**, **squeezing** it, suffocating her, **darkness** fading **into** liquid black. Breath became hard to grasp, and a burning pressure mounted behind Noor's eyes. More air, more darkness. Then, revelation: A creature of living dead shadow and **a thousand tentacle-like** appendages. A creature with a thousand burning, yellow **eyes** and a mouth of flame and blood. A creature wrapped in and out of Noor's thought, Noor's mind, Noor's soul. A creature dragging Noor into nothingness.

Fear overwhelmed her. Noor tried to run, to break free from the creature's asphyxiating grip. But the creature overpowered her and dragged Noor deeper and deeper into the night. Soon the agony roar of the men and women were no longer audible. Soon their torch fires had been **snuffed by indelible** darkness. Desperately, struggling for breath, Noor tried to fight. She bit and clawed, but, in the dark **silence,** her body had no strength. She tried to find, but her soul had been leached from her. Noor felt, a certainty, unable to move. Then, suddenly, like a door slam

of the forest. She depleted her strength and resources further. Furthermore, **staying** in the cottage also seemed at times to be the safest **course** of action. Here at least they had their supplies, food, etc. Here they **could conjure** the forest to protect them. Here they knew where they were. Out in the open, they would be horribly exposed, not only to unknown dangers and **fickle weather** but also to the Asterye. So, at times, feeling a dull need to do something, but rather added dangers to Noor and her mother's situation. Thus, Noor and her mother remained cloistered in the cottage, Noor in a constant state of paranoia, restlessness and anticipation, while her mother remained in a state of **seemingly unconcerned** sadness. It was all Noor could do to keep her hopes on her mother's **improvement and** not resign to losing that **outcome**.

One evening, two months after the attack, Noor sensed the presence of a lunar being near the cottage. Noor was sitting alone by the fireplace, cooking a medley tray of **nettle, fiddleheads and** garlic. Suddenly, her mother already in bed for the night, then, suddenly, she could of a lunar's presence filled her being. Noor froze. A wave of fear and panic began to swell over her. It's the Asterye, she thought. It's over. Be calmed Noor down. But then, dread in deep, she steadied herself. She stopped the **reflexive** surge to defensive action and stood. Now, to avoid her attention drawn to the sudden noise, she could sense her mother, and to keep it out of her **suspicion** and remain hidden to the being, leant in to the reality around her.

recognizable. Getting louder in my mind. Clearer. I had heard it before. It's beauty mesmerizing. Comfortable. A song of profound meaning which I had forgotten, returning now. Gently. Accompanied by images. A woman's face stained with lichens, eyes kind as the sun. A feeling of warmth and safety. The song now glowing on the vegetable woman's lips, getting louder in my mind, growing vivid. Chairs in the firelight. Stew over the fire. A hand on my shoulder. I yielded to it, grateful for the comfort. Grateful for the hand, for the song. I yielded to it, as it asked me to. Sorrow receding. Loneliness fading, burned away by eyes warm as the sun. Then someone taking my hand, again this vegetable woman with mossy hair, my mother, smiling, singing, but turning now, leading me on. Leading me deeper. I followed. Something on my lips. Something in my throat. I followed as it asked me to, the song becoming tangible as I turned, as I began to sing. I remembered it now. This song of protection. This song of healing. This song of power. Words formed in my mouth. Words, but not words. Syllabic sounds that seemed to ripple out of the melody like spontaneous shapes, like light. A path formed. A path of vapor. My mother on it, leading me deeper. I followed as she asked me to. Through valleys of fog. Over rivers of stormy cloud. I followed until she stopped. Until she turned, the song growing dim on her lips. Eyes like the setting sun, her face growing indistinct. I reached for her. But I could not follow. Everything dimmer now, translucent. The dark returning. The dark flooding back like the tide. Her gone. I could not hold it. I couldn't remember. The

mother's song, would likely have been fatal to con-
template. So whatever it was that initiated and guid-
ed the change, whether by some aspect of herself that
remained **unknowably** outside of conscious awareness or
whether by some **external** agent with an interest in
this world, it also kept her protectively unaware of
the doors of the process. So, little by little, she
lost herself, yet remained alive as she approached
some unforeseen conclusion to her ordeal.

The answer seemed to lie in the periods of lu-
cidity, which, as time passed, seemed to occur more
and more frequently. Initially **these periods** were
brief and far between. Noon could tell by the ravages
of her body the relative duration of the periods **of**
unconsciousness. But, as **the intervals between** in-
stances of lucidity shortened, so did the severity of
the physical pain and **baffling confusion**. While, at
first, it was not uncommon for Noon to awake and find
herself covered in snow or fallen leaves, or to dis-
cover a faculty of timber resting in her snotted and
mined hair, with every limb of her being ablaze with
pain, often now she came to to find herself standing
not far from where she had last awoke, or walking
along the shore of a lake she now recognized from the
recent past.

But none realizing that the beginning dates of
her lucidity were **the diminishments of** physical pain
as signaled by a decrease in the debilitating inten-
sity of the song of the trees. More often now, she
could listen in awe to listen to the **song** for longer
periods, and to remain awake sometimes for days at a

the earth and covered him. Then I dug three more graves and buried the family one by one. Finally, prayed for the peace, ... of each of there ... to the ... and ... of earth. But once more, before I could take myself leave, I knelt beside Nial's grave and wept. I wept and wept. I wept for Nial, for myself, and for my home . I wept ... I thought I would break and then somehow, I wept once more. When I was utterly spent, I collapsed and lay on the freshly excavated ground, staring up at the sky for hours and hours. As night fell, I pulled myself close. Huddled in my warmth, I slept out in the open, next to the ... mound of Nial's grave, and afeared of nothing.

When I awoke, it was early morning. The sun was low, throwing wide beams of golden light through the waving leaves. Immediately, I stood up, and shook from my body the remnants of the night's slumber. I also shook off the fragments of fresh grief that still stuck to my soul. Then, without further hesitation, I found the tracks of the possessed bear and ..., coming through the forest at my fastest pace.

The trail left by the bear was distinct and ... . Obvious damage to the undergrowth, a ... of the bear's ..., meant I hardly had to pay attention, though I wondered if it was the Archetype's ... dominance, the bear's ..., or the bear's resistance to domination that was the cause. In any case, following was easy, and I ran, pushing myself

against her paralysis. But it was no use. She could-
n't shake the power of the Archetype's gaze.

Instead, compelled, as she was, to watch the
Archetype's slow approach, and to read, as she slept,
she would be, to interpret in detail, every excruciat-
ing moment of her god-ordained and tortured death, too
real the weeping. But even the tears couldn't come.
Somehow the Archetype could prevent even that re-
lease. So Hoot's mind drifted toward her mother.
With the creature's amorphous tentacles encircling
her, she longed to be in her mother's arms one
last time, to feel her mother's love just once more,
to know the kindness of a final time that one can
find stored away for her throughout her life.

But then, at the very moment Hoot would have
been taken, something happened. Something strange,
something inexplicable, something so extraordinary
that the creature's arms never touched her, never
trapped her in their evil coil, never trapped her in
the endless clutches of the creature's despairing
vicious maze of looping death. Instead, the Arche-
type suddenly vanished. Gone, just like that. In
a horrified horror that edged so slowly to her, as, Hoot
watched at the floor of the cave, open and unsur-
faced the creature it all burst. She watched as the
building, the floorboards fell away en masse, re-
vealing a dark pit that opened ever wider. In the
ceiling, and into the entangled and earthy holes of
her mother's lair all the flared into nothingness,
disappeared as at once they fell and trapped
themselves around the Archetype and buried it, all of

Huge smoking discolorations covered

the distance,

I emerged from

headlong

fields

the clump of thatched

shadow

loomed

But on I went,

didn't have time to wonder. Quickly, Noor closed her eyes and resumed the song.

Again, the connection; then, moment by moment, impressions of increasing detail. Within the woman's madness, Noor felt a multiplicity of dreads that interwove fears of death, loss, judgment, and punishment. These combined with fears of the unknown and of the witches, themselves. Because Noor had never been exposed to the human heart to such a vivid degree, she couldn't tell if it was a common state of mind for human visitors, or an anomalous one. Whatever the case, Noor also felt other emotions, beneath the fear, desperation leading to defiance, torment of pride, outrage and determination.

These impressions seemed odd to Noor. Although she had on many occasions witnessed the distaste humans had for the pair of witches, Noor had never imagined nor felt inclined to imagine that the distaste would twist itself into something like heroism. Now that she was able to experience these feelings, she wondered if every supplicant had in fact felt a degree of self-congratulatory bravery as part of the ritual. Perhaps, the need to see heroism was in fact what engendered the distaste in the first place. Humans had to imagine danger where there was none, rather than admit weakness and vulnerability in the face of real danger, against which they were powerless. Nevertheless, the grief, the abject desperation which had ultimately given rise to the woman's outrage felt odd, deflated. At first, Noor had a difficult time gauging the totality of her cynicism especially since

... echoes ... vague in detail, ... like the aftershocks of ...

... purling ... heavy-leafed ... sharpness ... my mind ... my teeth ... I continued ...

... a dawn-gray ... scream ... battering the sensorium of my body. ...

determination, the **scars** on her skin glow no so oddly. Step by deliberate step, she neared the monster, hands **balling into fists** of rage that streamed with blood from **bite marks** I had somehow inflicted in the throes **of my wild agony**. But I couldn't feel her anymore, and I couldn't hear her thoughts. I had lost her. She had become all.

So I watched. It was all I could do. I watched as she walked into the creature, piercing its shadowy exterior and entering the structure of its presence. I watched as she stood in the center of the monster's form, spreading her arms, the light of her heart breaking through the darkness of the Archetype's shell. I watched as **an expression of** unbearable pain spread across her face, which then grew rigid and distant beneath the **gathering** of the light. And I watched as the **light** brightened and brightened, filling the cottage with the **fullness** of her power and her love, until I had to look away, blinded by the sheer **intensity** of that glow that followed. And so I watched until **it was done**.

..., below. And then, it was gone. A sudden quiet filled Noor's **mind** as she became aware that she could ... again, could speak again, could ... a low ... of sorrow and ... left her throat and ... into the bottomless black of the silent pit.

... , ... not over. Noor was **still** in ... danger, for the townsfolk, ... their fear, were now ... against the house. They ... town after ... **through** the **shattered** window and open doorway of the cottage. ... the ... of the ... were ..., and ..., ... stand in the doorway to the ... room and ... left of the bedroom, was trapped. The **flames** were too ... to escape through the front door. ... ... would ... out that way, ... they ... ... would ... the ... the appeared outside. There was no other exit, except through the ... wall of the bedroom, but the ... had gone.

Or was it? After ... over ... that ..., Noor ... ... **overhanging** the ... and ... ... to the ... of the house. Noor, ... to the door against the ... wall, ... and ... the ... ... the ... the ... ... Here, as the ... and ... ... lowered her, Noor stopped and ... at the ... ... of the ... with her ... ... The ... of ... the ... ... and Noor a ... to the ... appeared, the wood ... away, ... rotten ... Noor's ... ... and ... ... But Noor had ... to the ... ... , ... into the **hole** and ... of a ... ... of ... ... to the house.

Strange ... considering the only other ... meaning ... could persuade a human to ... possess multiple entities simultaneously. ... the prospect ... of ... an army? ... wherever it led ... would ... if I had my way, ... end ... in ... a human ... I knew

"An Archetype," Noor repeated thoughtfully. She had never heard of the creature, but now she was getting annoyed. Nothing her mother said made any sense and she kept ignoring Noor's questions. It was making her panic. She had never seen her mother like this, moving so frantically in preparation of a visitor. And she had never been ignored like this. It was even more terrifying than the dream itself. "Please, I beg you," Noor pleaded. "What is going on?" Finally, hearing the fear in her daughter's voice, Noor's mother stopped her frenzied activity.

"I'm sorry, my daughter, but he will be here soon," she said. Then, with speed, she returned to her work, swiping the scattered flower petals from the table to the floor, and covering the tray of seeds with a cloth that she then shoved into a drawer. "It will be all right, but we have to be careful."

"I don't understand. Careful of what?" Noor repeated, dismantling the light loom and placing it in a corner of the room.

"Just careful," she explained. Again, Noor's mother paused for a moment. Seeing the perplexity on Noor's face, she continued, "I'm sorry, Noor, I don't have time to explain, but I need you to listen. You can't be in this room when he arrives. I want you to go to the back room and stay there, okay?"

"Okay," Noor agreed.

"Good. Now, go. I will call you when it is over." As Noor stood in the doorway to the

... the ... of the A... ... ...

... of such loss, of such danger. ... a single ... of ... Power, ... creature in the room. ... in the doorway ... of her mother's passing. ... recognition ... Looking ... appeared ... accelerated ... Looking ... grimly.

"... ," ... hissed ... Looking ... ... power of the A... ... ... its human skin ... and burning teeth. ... Behind ... dead ... grass ... Looking ... ... seeking contact with ... Looking ... the glow, ...

appendages, and the **burning maw** of fire, bleeding flame and evil, glaring at me. Again, it hissed and tightened its grip around my throat. Again, it screamed and squeezed as it drank my thought, my mind, my soul. Again, it dragged me to its cage of nothingness.

I was overwhelmed with horror. Desperate, struggling **for breath, I tried** to fight. I fell and clawed, but, in **the black silence,** I had no strength. It had all been leached from me. **I fell,** drained of power, **unable to resist** the creature any longer. Then, suddenly, **like an axe** falling, my mind snapped shut and I was gone.

.   .   .

Daylight. Quiet. **My warm tongue** licking my face, my snout nosing gently at my ears. Thus, I woke to the warmth of my living breath. Then, abruptly, the onset of inexplicable horror **intermixed** with excruciating pain, cries, tears. I moaned in suffering, my fur and skin burned **and pacing** anxiously, **aimlessly a few meters away.** I whimpered and looked at myself with uncertainty, horrified by the dark stains of death on my skin. But, worst of all, lying on my side, covered in fear and agony around my weakened state, **I felt** abandoned; **I felt** death.

I tried to sit up. Pain exploded through my whole body, and I cried out, shattering me. Fear shattered along the surrounding of skin and tissue, where I curled in fear and trembled. But the wave of pain passed, and soon **I was** able to clear my mind to

lovingly at her daughter. I felt Noor's body relax as her mother's **hands slid** up Noor's arms to hold Noor's shoulders, then around her back, drawing Noor close to her chest, taking her in a deep embrace.

Noor, closing her eyes, leaning into the hug, gave herself fully to the moment, **to the fulfillment of impossibility, to the realization of a hopeless wish.** Here now, Noor allowed herself to drift into sensations of happiness, and to lose herself within them. I watched with worry as her awareness began to grow vague. A kind of darkness, like the onset of sleep, had begun to fill her mind. Then, wave upon wave of blissful, comforting sleepiness washed over her. Noor, she was on the brink of oblivion. A moment later, she was unconscious.

I had lost contact with her. But I knew what was happening. Without hesitation, I leaped up the cottage steps, and slammed into the closed door of the cabin with the tripled force of my body. The door broke open, and I fell into the room where Noor and now the Archetype, **a balled mass of shadow with one** tentacle wrapped around Noor's **throat**, stood. Seeing me, it exploded into a myriad arms that slashed and ripped, tore and thrust, as they tried to do me. Yet, despite the wounds and tears of the thrust, I pounded them. And I shattered. I lunged and bore. Whatever it did, it could not get ahold of me. But that hardly mattered because my plate did nothing. As much as I attacked the creature, my teeth only bashed through it as though it weren't there. To them, eventually, I would lose. Eventually, I would

"Sorry.

[redacted] known what the A[...] [...] about [...], that it really had a[...] [...] I never would have let you stay so long. I allowed you to remain because I thought it would benefit your education, especially since A[...] are generally [...] to but not very dangerous. [...] I'm sorry. It's all my doing."

[redacted] Mother. You didn't know."

"Yes, but now that we've [...] touched by it, everything is different. It may be able to [...] to weaken me, to weaken us, further."

"But it's gone [redacted] Plant. We destroyed it."

[...] mother did not respond. Instead, her eyes remained fixed on the ceiling, her face expressionless.

"Mother," [...] probed.

"Yes, [...], at least, it's gone...for now," she said, forcing her lips to smile. "But I do not think it was destroyed."

"But, Mother, it exploded. I saw it."

"[...], what you saw was an illusion. You you thought it was the Plate [...], it well [...] then, but it worked perfectly. Yes, you damaged it, destabilized it, even. But destroyed? It would not [...] if it were destroyed."

"How."

"We'd feel it," [...]'s mother said flatly.

"You mean, we feel the way we do now because it

The pair entered the warm light of the cottage, taking seats by the fire. Before another word was spoken, the woman began to weep once more. Noor let her. Tending to a pot of tea she had hung over the fire, Noor quietly and patiently bore the woman's weeping, once more taken by the genuine depth of the woman's sadness. When the water began to boil, Noor took the pot from the fire. She then added a blend of calming herbs she had gathered from the forest and cleared of moonlight the week before. She also began to sing softly.

Soon enough, the woman's tears slowed, and Noor handed her a cup of tea. Again, she waited, singing softly, as the woman sipped the brew and grew quiet. Minutes later, the woman had ceased crying altogether. Sitting humbly in the chair by the fire, she now regarded Noor with soft, imploring eyes.

"So, what has brought you to me." asked Noor, using the language of the townsfolk.

"It is my son," said the woman. "He's only a few months old, and he's dying." But this time, the woman did not cry. This time she did not weep, though sadness and horror flashed across her face

"How do you know." asked Noor dreamily

"I know," the woman said defensively. "I'm his mother."

"You misunderstand me," Noor responded softly. "I am asking you to tell me how you know so that I may know. Bring it to your mind."

away. It was unpleasant to watch his agony. I wanted to soothe him, but he needed to calm down so I could free him. But he kept pulling and pulling at the cord binding him, crying out in pain and fear, afraid of what might befall death.

"Be still," I said in a calm voice. "I will help you." But the cord was too tight on me, and the sound of my voice was too much to him. He began to weep in fear. His body shivered and trembled. I thought he might be out of his mind.

"Boy, be still!" I said again, more forcefully this time. "I will open the cord." But he would not wait. He would not understand how that I could do this to help. That is, or cured with a fear of death, his every instinct in opposition, rage turned to fear and confusion. So, rather than allow me to cut the rope, I could see a boy, a child, in the agony. Although that and not me to be so, at least, I stopped so that I could attend to his every request.

But the boy did not see it that way. He did not want to try and release himself, and I could not see with a spear on me and needed to be or be free while I was the one cause of his agony. He was troubled and crazed, out there and want me to cut my face and hands. He struggled so, he could go and be crazed. He even tried to bite me. But I was too strong for that. There I was on it, said again and was troubled, weary, one thing now, he was troubled and it could be done so. But he was too...

grew more firm in its touch. Young Noor was aston-
ished. ▮▮ threads of the mycelial network were
reaching out to her, caressing her hand softly, cool-
ly, in response to her reaching heart. ▮▮ fibers of
▮▮▮ intermingled with Noor's fingers, and suddenly
the vastness of the forest opened up to her. Sudden-
ly, she could hear birds singing from the treetops at
the other end of the woods. Suddenly, she could see a
thousand sun-dappled days really rushing between a
myriad lakes and streams. Suddenly, she could hear
the talking and singing of the trees. Their song was
familiar, like the entities' Song of Power, ▮ ● ▮ it was
also strange and more haunting, a melody more an-
cient than memory. Noor was lulled by it. So beauti-
ful, it made her want to sleep, to disappear, to live
in dreams. Yet it was also full beyond the fullness
of love, and it made her want to weep and to wail at
the same time. It made her want to live and die all
at once.

Just as suddenly as it came, it was all over.
Noor opened her child's eyes. Her mother regarded her
with attention, with all the emotion Noor had felt in
the earth a moment ago held there in her mother's ex-
pression. For a long moment, they looked at each oth-
er in silence, no one talked. A gentle wind blew over
them. The forest whispered.

▮▮ ●● ▮▮ now you can begin to understand, that is
who you are and where you come from, and that is why
what we are all a god to you." Noor said nothing more
only. There wasn't anything that could be said, she
now thought, only things to be understood. All the rest

couldn't guess.

As I came upon the next site of the Archetype's
entry, I found no further resolution to my misgivings.
Prior to the Archetype for an additional hundred me-
ters or so, now well within the realm of humanity, I
came upon another forest road, nearly as wide and
also much closer to the human settlement. Here I found
three transport carriages full of goods, either return-
ing from or going to the locale the Archetype was
leading me towards. On this occasion, however, the
creature did not seem to be as brutally thorough as
it had been at the previous site. First, the destruc-
tion was less complete, the carriages remained fully
intact, and the cargo mostly freed. Yet goods were
everywhere. All over the road and in the surrounding
road, the remains lay the corpses of men and the car-
casses of horses. I even found the bodies of a few
men that had been ordained along as lookouts and
pets. But this time they weren't mutilated into un-
recognizability. Rather, they each bore the clear
markings of the soul-drained creatures I had come
across before, the same markings I carried on my own
body.

Thus, it seemed, the Archetype, seeing the op-
portunity, stopped here and fed. Though it had drained
deeply, it had also done so cleanly, taking the sus-
tenance of its engorgement out of the ones too alone
to fight. In utter contrast to the previous site, the
bodies here seemed to lay where they had been killed.
The Archetype had done nothing to alter the scene.
Again, this seemed suspicious to me. Why would the

the proximity of ... the proximity of ... the proximity of

fallen leaves, twigs breaking in the dark, and the sound of ... accuracy of ... mother was ... empty ... by the fire.

... inside ... the empty chair ... this final process, ... departing ...

what remained found _____ _____ in
the morning light, the last of __ rose from a bed of
moss and slipped into the _____ shadows of the woods
on _____ padded feet. Then, I should have faded into
_____. Then, I should have been gone. But I was
_e_ __, _____, __ that spot, beneath a golden canopy of
_____ leaves, within a loveliness of song, for a mo-
ment longer than was possible. There, I lingered, and
there I stay as the dark hardened around the strained
figure of a woman standing with outstretched arms,
roots forming at her feet, branches springing from
her fingers, _____ to the leaves, singing, until
the dark covered her mouth with silence, the eternal
song of the Trees.

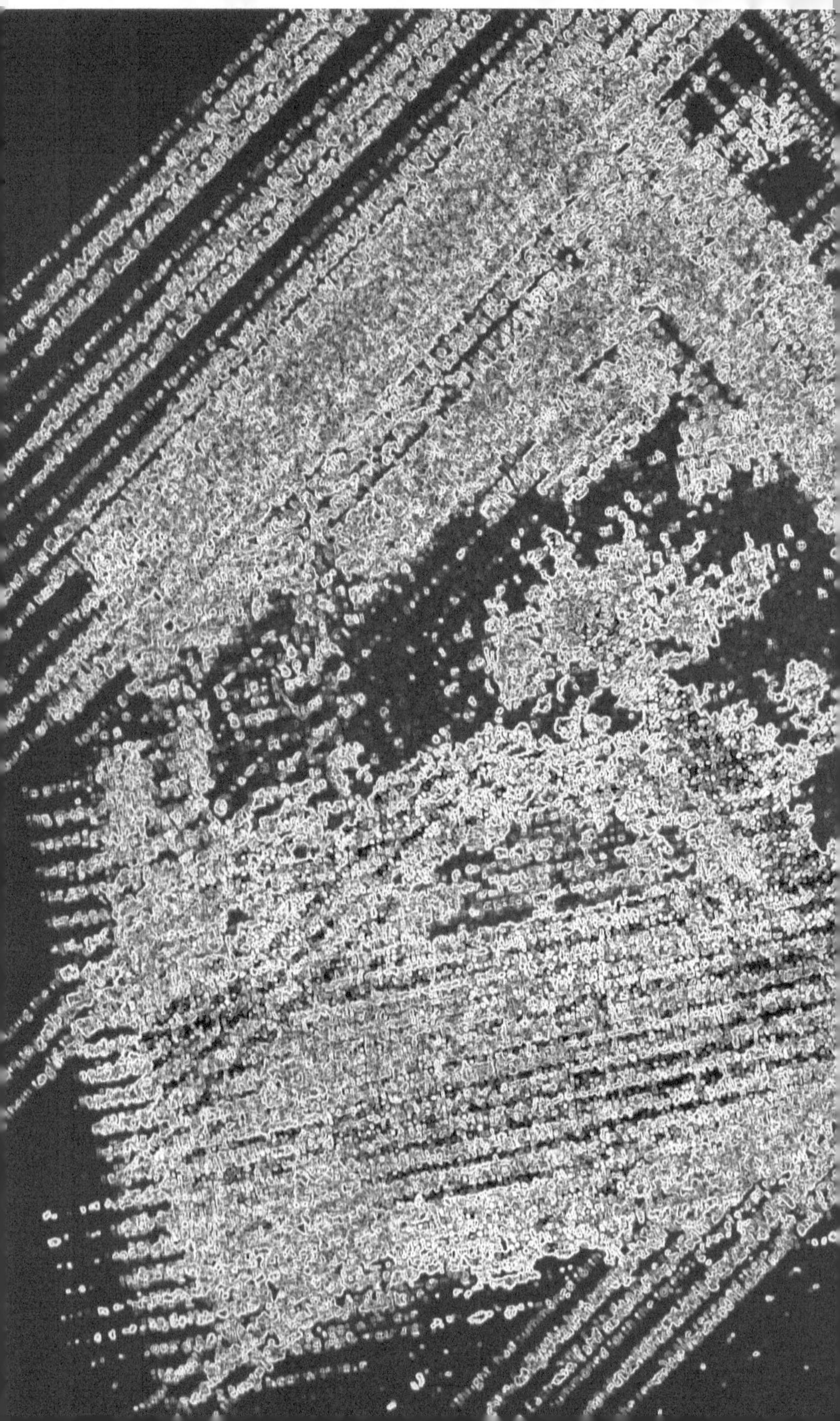

... to ... ..., ..., to atomize. Cell by cell, ..., ... of the ... ..., ...'s ... ... the specificity of the scene began to fade as ... ... to ... ... of being multiple and distributed, ..., ..., ...

... ...

... wasn't until after two years of almost non-... ... that ... ... to ... ... of ... day out of ... . But ...'s ... ..., ... and ..., ... began again to ... ... and preparation for the A...'s ... ... refit the door to ... ..., replacing ... ... explosion, ... with ... ... , every morning, ... Although ... and ... ... to hide ... ... bed-ridden, ... grateful to ... ... to ... ...

But, ... of all, ... the A... ... had not returned. ... of ... ... before ... and ... ... worry,

But that was all I could discover, and, frank-
ly, as I returned to my pursuit of the bear, glad to
leave this site of abomination behind, it was all I
could endure. Even though I had had three encounters
with the creature, it was still hard to accept the
warped depth of its evil and the perverted thoroughn-
ess of its cruelty. As I examined the scene, the
sheer magnitude of the horror had obliterated, for a
time, all capacity to feel. The grief and madness I
had so recently endured faded to a dull numbness that
overlaid a defensive air of sensitivity to nature. And
that was it. Even anger couldn't break through. But
now that I had left, my mind and heart began to
clear, and I was able to think more rationally about
the situation.

Foremost in my mind was the reason for such a
bloody attack. Was the Archetype acting in spite? Was
it so angry I had again gotten away with my life that
it lashed out partially at the first living creature
it came across? Perhaps. But the attack lasted so
long. As I had discovered, it went on for almost half
a day. This struck me as odd. It seemed like a long
time considering I had likely weakened it considerably
its connection to the material plane of its birth. It
had taken a significant chance there and it had failed.
Although it had also weakened me by killing Lia, it
did not know if I was in pursuit or not. Considering
this, half a day around her slain dead body seemed
like a purposeful waste. But what other reason
could there have been? I couldn't imagine. And it
was it headed toward the human settlement anyway?

besides us?"

"This is a difficult question," replied Noor's mother. "Truthfully, Noor, I don't know. I don't know if there are other witches besides us."

"You don't know." replied Noor in real worry. To Noor's young mind, her mother knew everything. In fact, this might have been the first, though it wouldn't be the last, time she witnessed her mother admit some form of ignorance. In any case, it always made her feel uneasy when she did. This being the first time, it doubly so bothered her.

"I don't," Noor's mother continued. "You see; besides my mother and you, I have never met another witch, nor have I seen one. In all my years I have never been aware of the existence of another witch or experienced something that led me to have looked for any. So, yes, perhaps...."

"We're alone," Noor interjected, crestfallen.

"Perhaps. I can't say. Sometimes I feel some thing that tells me otherwise. We just may not be meant to know each other."

"That makes me sad," concluded Noor.

"Yes, it may be lonely," Noor's mother agreed. "But that is the life of our kind, even if we are the only two in existence." Noor's mother extended a... arm and brought Noor close to her. "But remember, even when you are sure you are alone, the feeling is an illusion. In truth, you are held in the great arms of Nature...always. That is the meaning of the mystical

...river which flowed around the ... village. The river was **broad**, at least half a kilometer wide, **slow, and deep**. ... could't be able to cross it with... out ... exposing myself to the ...'s arrows. The ... was **just too bright** Meanwhile, ... my **pursuers** ... opening ..., their door ... at my heels.

My heart **sank**. For the first time that ... my position seemed **hopeless**, that **I wouldn't** be able to **avoid** conflict with the ... But I knew that ... a **disaster** It was exactly what the A... ... wanted from me. If I ... or killed even one of **the** ..., there would be no way for me to ... be the A... ...'s **poison**. ... one ... that would ... whatever **mold** the A... ... **wished** to ... I wished to remain near the village. But, if the A... ... that there, I was ... was not going to ..., and ... to the ... to **its evil**. I had to get out of ...

... I could hear that ... into the village... and their ... the ... and ... were ... side of the ..., while the ... and their door ... the ... and ... I had to ... and ... if I wanted to escape ... myself or anyone else, ... I needed that the ... Down on the ... side ... of the ... half. To the ... and ... , the ... would have ... ed ... **approaching** me ... But ... ... to the east, the ... would be **thinnest** and...

...silhouette of...

...rubbish... ████████ ...and...

...████████... the vines ████████...

...████ wept....

...through her **mind**, as, eventually, Noor, humming the
song to herself, far from the home she would never
return to, **drifted** into the darkness of slumber,
drifted into the release of sleep.

   .   .   .

     Noor woke, still **heavy with** fatigue, to the
grey light of **dawn** dusting the understory. Night had
passed instantly, in the blink of an eye. Noor did
not recall the descent into slumber **nor any dreams**.
But now, as she wiped the sleep from her eyes, she
felt **the wet remnants** of tears — tears she had not
known she had shed **lingering** on her cheeks. Slowly,
the events of the previous night returned to her, and
slowly, Noor felt **the full weight** of her solitude.
Her mother was gone, and now, for the first time in
her life, Noor was utterly alone in the world, utter-
ly **unprotected**. Not knowing what else to do, Noor
curled up on her bed of moss and leaves and wept. For
many hours Noor remained in this attitude, letting
grief, fear and loss wash over her like the huge
storm-swept swells of a gentle sea. She cried and,
when the pain was greatest, she screamed, thought
about her safety. But eventually, Noor was **spent**. She
could keep no more, so she lay on the ground, **staring**
at the bottom of the forest's grey shroud, **drifting**
in and out of consciousness, missing her mother and
wondering what to do or where to go.

     By midday, Noor was fully awake but weak from
hunger. She decided to do something and began foragin-
g for mushrooms in **the hollows** of the fallen trees
strewn on the forest floor.

. I didn't care . In
, .
, . .
.

A of lightness took me.
, ,
and , I flew.
, ,
, , illed
. , .
an arrow aimed at . , .
, . , , .
, everything
silent and bright and beautiful
, ,
it brushed my face. █████
. Perhaps, . .

, , .
. Endless and viscous. Innumerable.
, , . .
█████ .
. .
. .
. , ,
I didn't resist. .
, .
. I let the dead
, ,

of the forest, I soon realized that whatever had hap-
pened here was long over, and the Archetype had fled.
Among the smell **of blood**, the bear's odor was weak,
and it seemed to emanate from a point beyond the for-
est path, somewhere far ahead of me. Cautiously I
emerged from the weeds and began to explore.

The first thing I saw was blood. It was every-
where, splattered on everything, spotting dirt and
stone, and trunk **of tree.** It was even visible on the
underside **of the leaves of the canopy** 10 meters
overhead. So thorough was the spray, so abundant was
the blood, I had difficulty imagining what could have
produced it. I would never quite know the answer.
While the blood was most certainly human — I had
smelled enough human blood to know its quality — I
could not find the body that was or the bodies that
were its source. Rather, I only uncovered bits and
pieces, a chunk **of liver** here, or the flayed fragment
of a crushed **skull** there, but never enough to put it
all back together again. I could only guess at what
had happened, which was essentially reduced to the
number **of the human or humans who were** on the
path when the Archetype arrived. Clearly, the Arche-
type, whose strength and hatred had remained unabat-
ed since our encounter, used the bear to pulverize
its victims into one contrade mixture **of flesh,**
bone and blood. Probing the area further revealed little
more, except that, along the frenetic violence and
mutilation that lasted upward **of half a day,** the
quality of the breathing suggested that there were at
least three or more victims in the attack.

tall, I wondered how I could have detected it from so far away. But I didn't wonder this for long because there was one that... intensity that caught my attention. There was something so familiar and inviting about it that I couldn't remove my gaze, ██████████ look away.

So I sat and stared for a good time, waiting for something to **happen**. I heard myself whisper and ...with impatience, fear and uncertainty, and I felt a profound sadness and longing fill my heart. Deep in my mind **vague** memories of a small farming village began to emerge. I recalled the ... a lower glowing gently in the night, the murmur of **conversation**, the ... to be ...ded, and the deep ... them and ... . Then, my memories mixed with **mixed with** my perceptions, and I was mesmerized. Though I tried to force myself back into the present, to kick and claw myself out of **distraction,** ██ • ██ • █ - •• ██ was too strong. At any moment now, I was sure something monumentally important was going to happen, and I

██ ▲ ██ • •• •• ▲ - ▲• • ▲ ██

Indeed, something happened, but it was not what I expected. Before I knew it, I watched myself emerge from behind the **brambles** and walk in a trance toward the cottage, my eyes fixed on the dimly lit window. ...a bang, I ...ed to myself, but I didn't respond. ...ran to me, growling and **yapping** and nipped my hand. Pain shot through me, and I ...ned and ye...ed. Then a streak of anger throbbed **in my heart.** Instinctively, I raised the other hand to strike at my head, but, before I could deliver ██ •• ▲ - ••• • ██

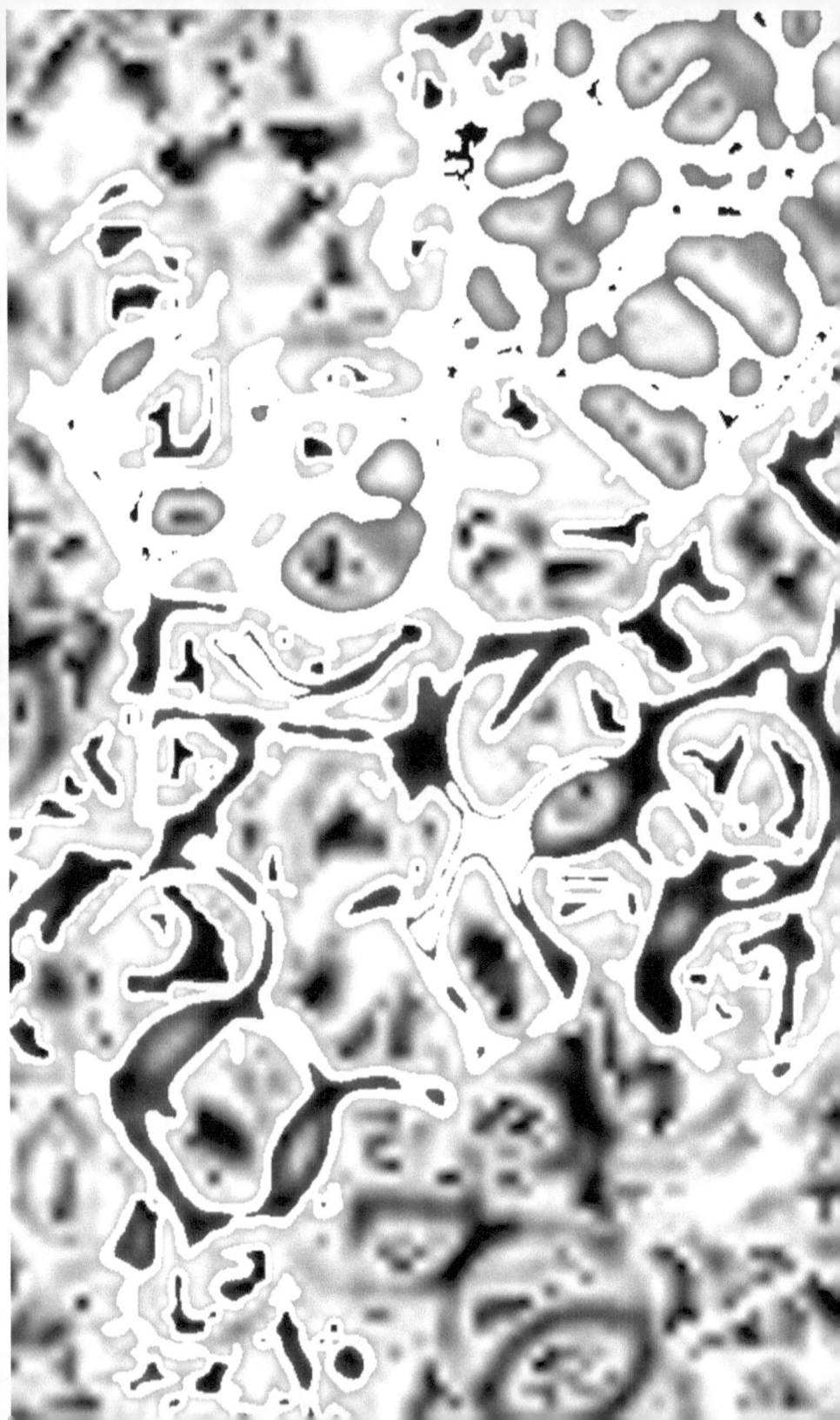

her, **something** strange. She felt her mother slipping from her grasp. She felt her stand before the Archetype, then she **turned and took** a step toward the oncoming door. She felt their power to regain her mother's will. She felt her mother's will go limp to her own **control** of her body, of her **movements**. As she walked toward the oncoming door, Noor's mother began to use the aura of Power to respond. Quickly, powerfully, the power flowed from her **voice**, moving throughout her body. In a moment, Noor's mother had regained control of herself. **Soon** she was again riding wildly in her chair. However, Noor felt her mother's fear. It was **a sea** of terror churning and roiling **in the pit of** her gut.

"Arius no," the creature roared. "You are right to fear, yet you remain yourself. I should like to know you better." Then, with a quick movement, the Archetype thrust its arm in Noor's mother's direction, grabbed her by the wrist. Noor felt the creature squeeze tightly. Pain shot up her mother's arm. Her mother tried to pull it free, but the creature's grip was too tight. Soon, the pain spread to her entire body, and then things began to fade. As all the energy that were being sapped from her body melted away, Noor's mother slid into agony and soon into **uncon-sciousness.** A moment later, everything went dark.

Something began to emerge in the darkness of Noor's mind. Vaguely, at first, like a cloud, then taking fuller shape on **the surface of** her awareness. In the **distance** and though she were looking through a

through the trees, while the light of the full moon
danced and pooled at the entrance to the hollow. Sur-
prisingly, I felt restored. Much of my strength had
returned and I was able to stand and walk with little
effort. I again went to the entrance of the tree and
looked inside. The interior was dark, but I could
still see the outline of Njal's body, a vague and
crumpled mass, lying motionless on the ground, beside
the other corpses. I resolved to bury him as soon as
the sun rose. I resolved to bury the family, too.

But for now, I would let them rest where they
lay, while I stood at the mouth of the hollow and
listened to the night air. Life had quickly returned
to this part of the forest. Crickets and katydids
chirped from the branches of the surrounding trees.
Fireflies sparkled here ███ ██. ██ dipped and
darted, feeding on invisible insects. I was grateful
for their company, but I was also ███████ something
had changed. I could only sense that somehow, as re-
sult of the confrontation, the area had been purged
of the evil, that somehow, perhaps by witnessing the
horror of what happened here, I had managed to trans-
mute it into memory, which I now carried with me.
Looking within myself, I could now feel the burden of
that memory, its soul-chilling brutality and evil I
was now forced to contain. Yet, the land had been
freed. It could now grow and live again.

In time, my mind returned to the events of the
over the days. It no longer seemed like █ accident
that I had come here, that I had heard the cry of

that time as me, Noor was never forced to confront
the full reality of her mother's **death.** But it was
different now. I could feel it. I could still feel
Noor, and I felt **the change** in her. She now under-
stood that her **mother** was murdered by the Archetype,
that, while she was distracted with a human visitor,
which the Archetype had used to find the cottage
again, the monster had **crept into** the bedroom and
drained her mother while she slept, dispelling all of
the protective magics as a result. Up until now, Noor
never had to reckon fully with what she had lost, nor
with how she had lost it. But suddenly she was bare
to the overwhelming pain of **her grief.** Noor collapsed
in pool of sorrow and rage as the full force of her
memories returned. Still, she thought, hadn't she
just seen her a moment ago. Wasn't that her on the
porch?

In an instant, I felt Noor's entire being latch
onto that possibility. That is the moment I knew she
had left me, and I would not be able to call her
back. **Even still, I tried.** Despite my heartbreaking
certainty, I beseeched her to return with all my
will. I begged her to consider the Archetype, the
likelihood of a trap. **But her mind** was closed to my
voice. She couldn't or wouldn't hear me, yet, for the
time being, I could still think her thoughts, feel
her feelings. There was still some connection there.
She *isn't dead*, **I heard her say** to herself. She are
alive! Somehow she escaped and now here she is. **Thus,
longing consumed her.** Thus, hope of saved Noor to eve-
rything except the belief that her mother was still

sky, that it was late afternoon. The ground was cov-
ered in shattered bodies.

"Is it dead," asked a young girl with a dirty
face and blood on her forehead. She had walked get-
ting closer to me than the rest of the townsfolk, yet
she did not seem afraid. In her hand was a knife
pointed down at the ground. "Did you kill it."

Immediately, I knew. Whatever had happened, I
was sure that I had been able to draw the Archetype
within me. Somehow, the scars it had left on my body
seemed all portals. But still, had I, no, I hadn't. The Ar-
chetype had been able to break the bond before the
absorption was complete. But now, our connection was
even stronger than before. Without effort, I knew the
direction it had fled for in my mind I could feel its
presence clearly. It stayed there like a sickness,
filling my thoughts with violence and blood.

"No," I said with difficulty, "it is not dead."
But I knew the Archetype had been weakened. However
disagreeable its presence was in my mind, I knew it
also meant it had been, at least partly, dissipated
and contained. Yet at what cost to me. It seemed that
now I bore it within me, and as I stood looking at
the townsfolk, a great hunger overcame me. I was weak
and needed help. I knew I could use their energy to
regain my strength. Then I might be able to chase the
Archetype and defeat it. It would be so easy. All I
had to do was reach out and drain them all. She was
only an arm's length away. She would be enough. At
least, that was what I told myself.

Noor closed her eyes and sang. Again, her mind was filled with the sound of weeping, but it was **louder now, closer.** The Lady of the Woods stumbled through the dark forest, labor breathing, **branches and briars** lashing the woman's **cheeks and legs** as the protective foliage that allowed the cottage readied to give way in the face of true need. There were familiar noises and **sensations,** things she had experienced before, when other visitors had made their way to the cottage. But the **perceptions** were to her now with a... unaltered **vividness,** which she could see...

...that she could not... **to be restored,** had killed... considering the perceived coming of the Archetype's approach. That was a reassuring sign. Either it wasn't the Archetype at all, or she could now perceive it, which meant she was stronger, perhaps strong enough to challenge it.

Yet there was more that was strange about this visit, unique even. Astonishingly, she could sense a feeling, for the first time, that seemed to be the emotions and physical sensations of the approaching woman. With intense wonder, Noor felt a stinging sensation on the skin of her **shins and arms** where briars snagged. She noted the burning in her **eyes and throat** that came from too much weeping. She felt the pounding pain in the woman's heart and lungs as she ran breathlessly. For a moment, Noor broke the spell to open her eyes. She looked down at the bare arms and legs, amazed to find them noticed by the... of the cottage, her cheeks **chapped and raw with tears.** She didn't know what to make of it, but she

...no, ... something outside ... ...

... Again, p... ... ... the embrace of ... ... Much o... ... ... found a piece of ... ... , ... , and ... ... that ... ... severed ... ... they ... ... that even after ... was taken from me, ... Thus, ...

... ... three ... ... and ... ... out of ... ... to look at ... ... longer. ... ... to ... ... But ... ... If ... ... however, ... enough ... ... However, in reality, ... to the edge of the ... ... that ... ... the ... ... of the ... ... of the tree. There, ... , ... , ... , ... , and ... ... and ... , ... , until ... ... , and ... ...

.   .   .

... ... night ... ... awoke. ... ...

... And each morning, ...

... above all others ...

... shimmered then with ...

... the dawn chorus of ...

... last vestiges ...

...they, looking about it, ... seemed ...

...had been nothing ... the ... legitimate ... had

... of the ... village, ... a ... of ... to

...ly out of the **ordinary**. ... looking ...

...

...the **nature** of the ... king, ... had the

...

... **bobbing in the distance**, ... the

... the **voices** of the approaching villagers, ...

cries, ... She now saw the

... **lay exposed**. ... all of

..., ... the obscuring

foliage ... to the ... At that ...

... the villagers ... **coming to**

destroy ... and ... ... the

... **no longer**. ...

...

weakest, consisting only of those tired men who had
been running after me all night.

But I did not have time to scout the accuracy
of this theory. Soon the torches approaching from the
north and east were visible. The men were closing
fast, their voices loud in the dark air. Before long,
their **dogs** had reached me, and they were now barking,
growling **and** yapping through the trees in front me,
but too frightened to attack. I didn't wait for the
cowman to arrive. I pointed to the line of torches
in the east. I did not know what I would find there,
but I planned on simply charging the line as hard as
I could, hoping to break through to the open woods
beyond. If I could do that without hurting any of the
men, then I would be able to escape without harming
my reputation and I wouldn't have provided any
"actual" evidence of my supposed evil.

Lucky for me, men are cowards. As head-long I
approached, I saw a line of five men (a line of five
torches really) directly before me. I didn't hesi-
tate. **I ran** right at them, growling and snarling and
shrieking **in my own way. Then, something perfect** hap-
pened. The men stepped aside. Seeing my manifold
strangeness was too much for them, and the multiplic-
ity of my movements was too frightening, so they
stepped aside. Or more accurately, they **fell to the
ground and cowered** and whimpered as I ran over them.
In any case, I broke through without incident and
without harm to anyone but myself. And I knew
that more men would be like the others. They would have
to hide their cowardice and fear, **but it didn't** mat-

███████████████ came easily to her. Not only had she heard the song every morning of her young short life, each time she began to sing, she felt it rise from somewhere essential in her being, like she was remembering it, not from her own past, but from eternity. It gave her ███████████████ in the world. It made ██████ **feel** like earth, the sky cool like sky. But more than that, it gave her a sense of power and agency. Through the feeling of love, she felt strength well up in her as together she and mother called forth the protective energies of the woods. She knew at **these moments** that she could do things others could not, that she could make things happen. She knew she had skill and ability. With her mother's guidance, Noor would spend these early days of her learning her mother's craft, assisting her in the daily cultivation of protective and healing magic. By the time she reached young adulthood, Noor would be a skilled and independent practitioner of her mother's art, though she'd remain an apprentice for years to come.

Inside, the cottage was comfortable and warm as befitted Noor's home. **A fire burned** constantly in a corner fireplace. The floor, though made of bare wooden planks, was clean and covered with lots of woven carpets. Tapestries of linen and wool and of woven flowers adorned the walls. A mushroom smell curled over the fire. Besides the living room, there was one other room, a bedroom which Noor and mother shared. Yet ███████ ●●● ● ● ● ███████ While the living room was also a workshop where mother and daughter labored together, the bedroom was

At first, it was comforting, not just to have something, anything, to do, but also because it was something she did most mornings with her mother, all the time they had tended to the protective needs of the home. However, while it was at first a solace, the pain of the memories soon overwhelmed her. Noor recalled how her mother used these foraging outings not only to gather food and medicines, but to teach Noor about both. Often, it irritated her, but now it brought Noor to the brink of tears.

"And what is no of mushroom is this is." Noor could hear her mother ask.

"That's an easy one, Mother," replied young Noor. "That's chanter's Cloak."

"Good. And what about this one," she asked.

"Lynx Paw," the witchling replied.

"And what is Lynx Paw good for."

"It has many uses, but it is an especially powerful key to the higher realm of enchanted souls," replied Noor. "But I don't like the way it tastes. Sweet, like candy."

"Yes, me, too," said Noor's mother with a smile, the day gathering a clusters of fungi and placing them in a basket.

So many memories were imbued in this act that Noor had unconsciously tapped the ability within a renewed sense of permanence. Like the ritualistic routine of a meal, Noor felt protected by the sanctity of orchestrated routine. But now, Noor's world was with

all .... one ....

Then, ..., I .... I .... of the body of the .... and out ..... the hollow of .... the ...., my .... cleared, ... of ... . growling around me. I became .... massive .... my snarling facets. .... coordinated ..... In an ...., ... the animal ... ..., ... the ...., ... Instead, I .... I begged for .. .., ... But .. .. how many wounds I ...., I ...., ..., ..., ..., ..., a bloodied foam dripping from ... ., ..., ..., ..., ..., ... Blood ... . my eyes ... ., ... I gagged ... ., .. I bit ... .

Then, ..., ..., ... o my throat. ... ... ▪▪ ...., ... at ...., ..., ... ▪▪ I tried to scream, ...

About Andrew Brenza

Andrew Brenza's recent books include the visual poetry series *The Book of Andrews* (Red Fox Press), the poetry chapbook *The Heathery Heart* (BlazeVOX) and the experimental science fiction play *Night Walking & The Makers' Taint* (Sulfur Editions). He is also the founder and editor of Sigilist Press, a micropress devoted to the publication of visual poetry.

About Unsolicited Press

Unsolicited Press is based out of Portland, Oregon and focuses on the works of the unsung and underrepresented. As a womxn–owned, all–volunteer small publisher that doesn't worry about profits as much as championing exceptional literature, we have the privilege of partnering with authors skirting the fringes of the lit world. We've worked with emerging and award–winning authors such as Amy Shimshon-Santo, Elisa Carlsen, Sommer Schafer, and Laura Gaddis.

Learn more at Unsolicitedpress.com. Find us on Twitter and Instagram @UnsolicitedP.